Malta
The Nurse of The Mediterranean

Albert G. Mackinnon

Alpha Editions

This Edition Published in 2020

ISBN: 9789354215964

Design and Setting By
Alpha Editions
www.alphaedis.com
Email – info@alphaedis.com

As per information held with us this book is in Public Domain.
This book is a reproduction of an important historical work. Alpha Editions uses the best technology to reproduce historical work in the same manner it was first published to preserve its original nature. Any marks or number seen are left intentionally to preserve its true form.

TO

FIELD-MARSHAL LORD METHUEN

G.C.B., G.C.V.O., C.M.G.

GOVERNOR AND COMMANDER-IN-CHIEF

MALTA

FOREWORD

By His Excellency Lord Methuen, Governor and Commander-in-Chief of Malta

IF the hospital arrangements have proved satisfactory, if the lives of 80,000 patients have been made happy during their time in Malta, a great amount of the credit is due to the philanthropic work carried out on the island.

What has struck so many besides myself is the unostentatious, quiet manner in which the help has been given — good organisation, no waste of the money so generously given.

There has been no friction, no overlapping.

The British Red Cross and St. John's Ambulance Societies, the Scottish Church,

Foreword

the Church of England Institutes, the Young Men's Christian Association, have one and all given a helping hand, and earned the gratitude of everyone in Malta.

Malta has been given a good opportunity for doing good, and she has faced the situation splendidly.

To no one do I tender my thanks more truly and warmly than I do to Rev. Albert G. Mackinnon, S. C. F. Presbyterian, one of the foremost leaders in this labour of love.

METHUEN,
F.M.

THE PALACE,
MALTA.
August, 1916.

CONTENTS

FOREWORD, BY HIS EXCELLENCY LORD METHUEN 9

INTRODUCTION 13

CHAPTER I
AT SEA IN WAR TIME . . . 19

CHAPTER II
MALTA HOSPITALS 40

CHAPTER III
A SAD MARCH PAST . . . 60

CHAPTER IV
THE LAND OF THE OPEN HAND , 84

Contents

CHAPTER V
MALTA RAINBOWS 103

CHAPTER VI
IN LIGHTER VEIN 126

CHAPTER VII
ORGANISATION 149

CHAPTER VIII
THE VALLEY OF THE SHADOW . . 166

CHAPTER IX
A SCOTTISH PICNIC 187

CHAPTER X
UNDER CANVAS 202

CHAPTER XI
CHRISTMAS IN MALTA . . . 216

CHAPTE RXII
RELIGIOUS WORK AMONGST THE WOUNDED 238

INTRODUCTION

MALTA has assumed the rôle of nurse. I ought perhaps to say *re*sumed; for when Filippo Villiers de L'Isle Adam took possession of this island in 1521 at the head of his Hospitallers, the Knights of St. John of Jerusalem, one of the first things he did was to build a hospital. With the Crimean War and Florence Nightingale nursing became a new profession for women, and Malta had a foremost share in those epoch-making days, when women found a rallying place beside the flag as well as men.

Never in her history, however, did Malta reach forth her arms, bared for the task, to receive such a burden of suffering humanity, the human wreckage of battle, as in the summer months of 1915. It is to tell you the story of these days that this book is written. I want to bring you with

Introduction

me into these packed wards, where the air, despite the best ventilation, is heavy with the smell of iodine and the sickening odour of lacerated flesh, where men silently grapple with pain or their last enemy death.

In the latter days of May I found myself in the stream of skilled men and women who were hurrying East to help our stricken heroes to fight and, if possible, win this struggle in the wards, one that demanded greater powers of endurance than the conflict of the trenches. The surgeons had their instruments and their medicines, the nurses their training; the British Government sent me and other chaplains because it believes that "man doth not live by bread alone."

The following chapters are sketches drawn from life, glimpses of wards and men as seen by the eyes of a chaplain whose sacred privilege it was to walk a little way with our sufferers in the dark valley, and to hear and see some things that it is not lawful to repeat, and others that it is well the world should know.

Introduction

The pronoun " we " often recurs in these pages, and the reason is that on the day I received the short summons to go the " we " decided not to separate, but that husband and wife would go together, although the future had great uncertainties. Thus as chaplain I was able to carry on a dual work ; one half of me—the better half—cutting and buttering bread in the morning and making tea in the afternoon for the thirsty soldiers who sought the shelter of our Club ; while the other half was in the wards whetting the appetite of recovering men by telling them what grand teas they would get when they were able to limp abroad.

I stepped into a growing organism when I landed in Malta. Like mushrooms hospitals were springing up everywhere, offshoot buildings were becoming entities. Schools grew into hospitals in a night, and then spread round them their white skirts of canvas tents. But there was order and method in it all. . . . It was fortunate that at that moment there was at the head of

Introduction

affairs in Malta a Field-Marshal, whose genius for organisation had made him one of Britain's great generals. His Excellency the Governor, Lord Methuen, not only planned the construction of the rising camps, but kept a watchful eye on each detail, and by his constant presence in the ward encouraged the sufferer. Especially his ready sympathy and help towards all true effort was a great strength to those whose aims reached farther than the mere healing of the body. The religious workers knew and felt that they had a friend in the Governor, and everything that could be done to facilitate their work received his speedy sanction. His kindly Foreword to this book is but an illustration of his willingness to assist wherever it was possible, and as long as the tale of the Malta Hospitals is told there will live the gracious memory of the Governor who fathered the stricken sons of Empire placed under his care.

My gratitude is due to a number of magazines and newspapers to whom I am

Introduction

indebted for reproducing, in somewhat different form, much of the material first served to them in the shape of sketches. These include *The Scotsman, The Sunday at Home, The Westminster, The Christian Herald, The Christchurch Press, The Otago Witness,* and last but not least *The Greenock Telegraph,* for to this latter paper I am indebted for having any story to tell. Through the generosity of its publisher and Editor it opened its columns not merely to my articles but the need which they pictured, and its readers held out such a helping hand to Malta, that we were able to start and maintain our club for wounded soldiers, and on every week-day of the year provide for them a substantial tea free of charge. As you read the story you will learn how others joined in assisting the work, but we can never forget the one who gave the first shove off. I am also greatly indebted to Colonel Ballance for his kind assistance in procuring for me many of the medical facts mentioned in this volume.

CHAPTER I

AT SEA IN WAR TIME

WHAT one is not permitted to tell is, of course, the most interesting part of a voyage in war time. However, even when that is subtracted there remains enough to give piquancy to what otherwise is a commonplace experience.

The novelty of travel in these war days begins at the very start. The familiar hotel in London was unfamiliar in its inner aspect. In the hall a pile of soldiers' accoutrements was the first thing to meet the eye. Khaki overcoats hung from every peg in the cloak room, and graceful figures clad in blue with shoulder strap and star flitted about the rooms. These were Canadian nurses who had just arrived and

At Sea in War Time

were bound for the front. Very smart they looked. Their dress seemed to be fashioned after the pattern of the American officers' uniform. Most becoming it was, and there were plenty of stars. So many, in fact, that they all seemed to be superior officers, and one wondered where the private came in. Perhaps in this contingent there was none, and all these capable-looking young women were meant to command instead of obey. A duty for which none appeared unequal.

The boat train first brought home to us that we were bound for foreign parts, and that on the railway platform the pathos of war eclipsed its glory. Like canny Scots we had broken the regulations and stuck by our baggage in these uncertain times. Only light luggage was supposed to be taken on this express, and the porter who stepped forward so eagerly to open the door of our taxi opened more widely his eyes. But we had a clear conscience, and with that one can face even stern officialism. If there were thirteen pieces of baggage of

At Sea in War Time

all sizes we knew that their contents were not all personal. Many of them were filled with parcels of generous dimensions for our brave soldiers in the East. The thoughtful generosity of friends sent us not empty-handed away, and it is reassuring to carry not merely a message of comfort on the lip but a token of sympathy in the hand. Thus were we armed, and so red-tapeism lost its terrors. It was represented by an official who was prepared to weigh small baggage, and who looked at the growing pile on the porter's barrow with dismay. How we got past him need not be told. Veteran travellers will guess, others must learn by experience. I had secured our porter as an ally and he worked wonders, and what did not go into the van went into the carriage. We had gone early and so chose an empty compartment.

We were not, however, to have it to ourselves. We had just got ourselves comfortably ensconced when two Indian nobles were ushered in. They were dressed as British officers, and wore khaki turbans,

At Sea in War Time

and were returning from the front. Fine specimens of Indian gentlemen they were, most courteous in manner and agreeable as fellow-passengers. There was a third who joined the others later, and the trio were an object of interest throughout the voyage. One felt a thrill of pride in our great Indian Empire as we looked on these Eastern princes who had so loyally drawn the sword in defence of the mother land.

At last we were on board the *Malwa*, and our thoughts went at once back to Greenock. The big ship as she lay in dock seemed too solid to be pitched about by the waves, but we had yet to learn the strength of the ocean. Even the *Malwa* was to stagger before the blows of the Atlantic.

Again there was a parting, and this time it was the last. Khaki-clad figures leaned over the ship's rail, and on the wharf stood groups of women. British courage perhaps reaches its height at such a trying hour. Small talk, like handy change, was useful that moment. The big things were behind. Within the heart was the unutterable,

At Sea in War Time

while on the lip was the ready sally. The women were not less brave than the men. Though tears were not far away, yet they were out of sight. Smiles hid them.

One of those insignificant incidents that sometimes happen relieved the tension. The gangway had been drawn, and imperceptibly the big ship was drifting from the wharf, the gulf which for some would never be bridged was already widening. At that moment a gentleman attempted to throw a letter ashore. It fluttered in the air for a moment, and then dropped short into the water. A rather burly policeman ran for a grappling iron, and his efforts to fish up the soaking envelope absorbed attention. It was a bit of delicate balancing, and sometimes he would have the letter almost within reach when it would drop back into the sea, and a humorous groan from deck and wharf announced his failure However he was nothing daunted. He had taken to heart the story of Bruce and the spider. Meanwhile the distance was steadily widening. At last a cheer went up, the voices on board blended for the last time with those on shore. The policeman had won! He was holding the dripping letter in his hands. Such was the final parting, and if the whole burlesque had been planned it could not have served a better purpose.

Usually one takes a casual glance at one's stateroom, and then thinks of food. But this was to be no ordinary voyage. The last papers put into our hands told of the sinking of the Elder Dempster liner in the Channel, by a German submarine, and it was rumoured that two were lying in wait for a bigger haul. Therefore an article that is usually kept out of sight on a top shelf became a matter of importance. How soon it would be needed no one could tell. This was the life-belt. The newer type is less intricate than the older one; but even the method of handling it has to be learned. So I got the steward to give me a lesson in the tying of the slip knot, and the right adjusting of this body belt—information which I was able to impart later to others.

At Sea in War Time

Next in importance was the introduction to the Captain with which Dr. Caird had so kindly furnished me. On a P. and O. Liner the name of its builder is one to conjure with, and it had immediate results. The place of honour on a ship is the Captain's table, but more to me than the honour is the information which is thus put within one's reach. The one man who knows what is going on is the Captain, and news on shipboard is ten times more valuable than in the land of newspapers. The smallest item is as food for a starving man, and is feverishly devoured by the ravenous passengers. Especially is this so on a voyage in war time when there are no Marconigrams except the naval messages which are meant for the Captain alone.

Hence it was a delight to find that we were especially invited to sit at the little table with the Captain, for the meals are served at small tables in the dining saloon. Here also were some most interesting people, the wife of a British Admiral going out to see her husband, an officer who had

At Sea in War Time

been wounded at the front and who had been given a Mediterranean command, a judge of the Supreme Court, and a lady, much travelled, whose son-in-law held a high position in the Greek army, and who was a mine of information on the Balkan States. The Captain, who was courtesy itself, and whose conversational art was to draw your opinion rather than give his own, chatted and chaffed with a ready wit, as if German submarines were not lurking for their prey. He did not, however, underestimate the danger, and when conversation turned to such a topic as life-belts he gave his opinion seriously.

No sooner had we started than we were reminded in an ominous way that the threat of the enemy was a reality. The boats were got ready and slung out on their davits. As I watched the Lascars at work, I realised that the launching of one of these big life-boats is not a thing which can be done in a moment. It took fully an hour before all the boats were made ready for lowering. Directions were posted up telling the passengers what to do in the case of being torpedoed. Those in the first cabin were to meet in the saloon with their life-belts on, and the boats would be loaded from the hurricane deck.

While on board every precaution was being taken against sudden attack in the Channel itself, vigilance was personified in the restless destroyers as they raced up and down splitting the waves with a graceful curl. One of these stopped us at the mouth of the Thames, and directions were given there as to our course to the next patrol.

At last we were under way, with our head down Channel and our screws driving us at sixteen to seventeen knots. We passed the slower going tramps, but soon we were reminded that we were not the fastest craft afloat. Hidden behind a curl of spray a destroyer came dashing up. It swept alongside, and a sharp, short command was shouted through a megaphone. Later its purport leaked out. We were ordered to make for a certain English port. Many

At Sea in War Time

were the conjectures as to the reason for this, and now that we know what it was it is better that it should not be made public. Suffice it to say that on Sunday forenoon instead of being well on our way we found ourselves in harbour. The excitement and distraction caused by what was taking place around us caused the Captain to forgo the usual service. All on board were on deck and too absorbed in the unusual scenes to be gathered together in the saloon.

Alongside of us lay a big liner which had just come in, and it was rumoured that she had rammed and sunk a German submarine. However, the Captain gave us later the tale by the right end. The submarine had chased and fired at her but she had managed to escape.

Again we were off, and soon we saw the shores of Old England dipping below the horizon, and we were settling ourselves down to the usual pastimes of a voyage, when suddenly the engines ceased, and all looked with a start towards the sea. A big wave and behind it two funnels belching smoke showed that another destroyer was racing towards us. It circled round our ship, another order was given, and the *Malwa* was put about and headed back to the port we had left.

There was no lack of conversation now, and conjecture was rife, what did it all mean? We counted seven explanations which were repeated as authoritative; but the men on the bridge kept silent. Later, when we got back to port and learned what it was, any grumble at the loss of time was silenced, and all felt happier for the guardian care of the British navy.

Once more we were off with a destroyer on either side, and it looked as if we were driving a tandem of spirited steeds. Their presence reassured us, and though many slept with their life-belts on their sleep was undisturbed.

Monday morning found us alone on the broad seas. There was a general feeling that danger was past, until at half-past ten the alarm bell sounded through the ship. Almost with the first stroke could be heard

At Sea in War Time

the tramp of hurrying feet, the men rushing to their posts at the boats. We seized our life-belts and along with our fellow-passengers hastened to the saloon. Here an animated scene presented itself. All had collected there, and everyone was busy fastening on their life-belts. What surprised me was that there were so many who had not learned how to adjust them. The method when known is simplicity itself, but it is very easy to make a fatal mistake. The pathetic touch was added by the sight of two little children, who had four miniature life-belts fastened round them, and who were looking in wonderment at this apparently new game.

Then the Captain came on the scene. The alarm had been given to test us and see what we would do in real danger. He examined carefully the fastening of each life-belt and pulled the slip knot to see if it were tied properly. Then he gave us all a few directions as to how we were to act if the alarm should again sound in real earnest.

At Sea in War Time

Such is life at sea in these perilous days. Its gaiety is not lessened. The deck games go on as before, but there is a sense of constant preparedness for a sudden emergency, for the innocent looking waves may hide a cruel foe. On each deck Lascars are constantly scanning the sea for sight of a periscope, and even the passenger's eyes are often lifted from book or deck quoits to cast a furtive glance at some breaking crest, which for the moment seemed like something else.

The eeriness of plunging through the sea in the darkness at seventeen knots an hour with lights out is one of the sensations of war time. It was equalled by the uncanny feeling one experienced in the improvised concert-room which had been erected one night on deck. For, of course, there must be the usual concert or else certain charitable funds would be the losers. Besides, we had more than usual reason for it on this voyage, for had we not on board the smallest man and woman in the world as well as the largest, and surely the tall, energetic man in charge of the troupe was the best showman that ever lived, so at least we all thought, including, I feel certain, the Indian Princes, who forgot their royalty in their laughter.

The concert hall would have been the open deck in normal times ; but how carefully screened it was now with canvas so that no chink of light might betray the passing of the liner. We got that night what the Australians and New Zealanders will be enjoying for months to come. The smallest man and woman had other gifts of entertainment besides their size, and the conjurer made one feel that there was no use passing round the hat, for he seemed to be able to draw everything imaginable out of his mouth, even money.

Nor must one forget Jones, the Bluejacket, who already had become the popular hero of the voyage, for other reasons which I cannot narrate. He sang a song and was cheered to the echo, and when he left the ship at Gibraltar there was universal sorrow.

I could not help thinking of the contrasts

PRESBYTERIAN CHAPLAINS IN MALTA.

Capt. Cowan.   Capt. Levack.   Major Mackinnon.   Rev. C. McEchern.   Capt. Menzies.

Photo by S. L. Cassar, Malta.

At Sea in War Time

that night. The merry company hidden under the shelter of the canvas, the anxious eyes on bridge and deck peering into the darkness, and somewhere out on the tossing waves, a half human serpent gliding stealthily along on our track seeking for a chance to drive home its fatal sting. Such is life, but I must not stop to philosophise.

Gibraltar in war time wore a sterner aspect than usual. I had just got out of my morning bath, and in my dressing gown stepped on to a quiet corner of the deck to view the frowning cliff of Britain's greatest fortress, when I saw the conjurer of the night before preparing to take a snapshot. But other eyes were watching, and an officer laid his hand on the upraised arm before the click of the shutter sounded. No photographs are permitted, and indeed the authorities are not very anxious about strangers coming ashore. We took a carozze and paid our respects to the United Free Church minister stationed there, and in turn were taken by him to see his church, and the new stained glass window presented

At Sea in War Time

by Sir Ian Hamilton. So the short sojourn quickly passed, and we left with a bird's-eye-view impression of this guardian citadel. It will be a daring foe that will ever attempt to bring down the British flag from that proud eminence.

The sail along the African coast was one of the most delightful experiences of the voyage. We came so near to land, that every house was visible, and the streets in Algiers were quite distinct. Then we bethought ourselves of Malta, and in the grey dawn I first saw the white cliffs gleaming out of the haze, with the surf wildly dashing against their foot. There was a heavy roll as our ship slowed down and steered for the narrow entrance to Valletta harbour, not without danger, for even here the enemy's submarine had been sighted. Then followed a scurrying of hundreds of little dghaisas, and in one of them, under a military helmet, I recognised the well-known features of a Greenock minister. It was a delight to hear the kindly tones of Rev. Donald Campbell's voice. Under his escort we were soon getting a taste of what is to be our every day experience, a tossing in the frail but skilfully manipulated dghaisas. We raced for the shore. Two fellow passengers bound for the Far East had accepted our invitation to lunch, and they and we were charmed with the rooms which Mr. Campbell had so well selected for us.

The Rev. Mr. Primrose, who had just returned from the Dardanelles, joined us also at lunch. Thrilling were the stories he told us of the terrible fighting through which he and our brave Scottish lads had passed. Our hearts swelled with pride as we listened to his account, though we have been greatly saddened by the news of Lieut.-Commander McKirdy's death. Already I have come across a number of the Anson Division lads, but must reserve their stories to later. We enquired at once for Lieutenant Fraser Brown, but learned that he had left again for the Front.

Someone remarked to me before leaving that if I were to see the bestial brutality of war I could never again preach a war ser-

At Sea in War Time

mon. I have seen something of its indescribable horrors already, too awful to describe. My heart melted as I stood by a brave man who was dying alone in a corner of a hospital, as his eyes glazed, and his bearded face took on the fixity of death. I remembered he was somebody's darling, and here was I a perfect stranger, the only one with him at the last. All this but deepens one's indignation at the war and the miscreants who in their foul passion have devastated homes and trampled under foot all that is noblest and best. To-day as my wife, Mr. Campbell and I stood by the door of one of the many hospitals here an ambulance drove up and a wounded officer was carried on a stretcher into the building. He had just arrived from the field of battle, the coat he wore was all splotched with blood. He had been shot in the eyes, and the ambulance man told us that he would never see again. Yet as they lifted him he made a cheery remark that caused them to smile. Such is a sample of the pathos and the pluck war reveals.

At Sea in War Time

Already the wounded soldiers are finding out our room, and the generosity of the kind friends at home is filling it in the evening hours with tobacco smoke. How these boys revel in the little touch of home life, and enjoy their tea! It would gladden the hearts of the donors of the gifts we brought to see how they are appreciated. Mr. Campbell has dubbed our two waiters "Henry the First," and "Henry the Second." They are ever smiling and ever ready, and are kept busy bringing hot water to fill the homely teapot. It is the womanly touch that is worth more than all a chaplain's words of counsel. It is worth the risk of submarine and heat, and I believe that the service rendered through the teapot, for the Maltese do not know how to make good tea, will do as much to comfort and help our Scottish and Colonial soldiers, as the more official work of the chaplain.

Nothing has touched me so much as the splendid spirit exhibited by our brave fellows. It is beyond all words. Not yet have I heard one word of complaint or even an acknowledgment of pain. But yet it is all inexpressibly terrible. I must reserve for another occasion the thrilling stories which already I am beginning to hear, and a description of this thoroughly eastern town which interests at every point. The faldetta hooded women, the straggling goats who seem to have a right-of-way on the busiest streets and pavements, the carozze men who dog your steps on the chance of a sixpenny fare, the swift dghaisas as they race across the heaving waves, for the waters round Malta never seem at rest, all give an air of novelty to surroundings that in themselves charm by their brilliant contrasts of colour. Through this maze of moving humanity passes the well-known figure of the Gaelic United Free Church minister of Greenock; though his people might scarcely recognise their minister under the shade of his big helmet, and as I watch him I feel that Mr. Campbell is a born chaplain. There is not a Greenock lad in Malta whose heart has not been warmed by his sympathetic grasp and words, and not a ward he passes through where a smile is not left on the soldiers' faces through his ready if pawky humour. As I write I seem to hear his voice as he took me on my first rounds, and said on entering each ward, " Are there any Greenock or Scotch lads here ? " and there would come an answer in perhaps a cockney voice—" Yes, sir, you'll find un in the heighth bed," and sure enough there is a face already smiling its welcome at the sound of a Scottish voice.

CHAPTER II

MALTA HOSPITALS

THE silence of Valletta in war time is what impresses the visitor. Not that it is silent. The cries of street vendors, and all the ordinary noises of a congested town added to the voluble talk of its inhabitants make sound enough; but even that babble is as silence compared with what Valletta used to be. The bells have stopped, and the world has not come to an end. From the vigour with which the hundreds of them used to be beaten from one quarter of an hour to the other, it seemed as if the place were making a frantic effort to avert some impending doom, and in the mind of the peasant this thought was not far away. The effort has ceased, and the heavens have not fallen.

Malta Hospitals

THE SILENCED BELLS

Napoleon tried to silence the bells of Malta but he failed. A British medical officer has thus accomplished what the great Emperor could not do. Colonel Ballance, with the sympathy of a true surgeon for the thousands under his charge, had the matter of the bells brought before His Grace the Archbishop of Malta. His Grace, with his usual readiness to assist all work for the wounded, ordered the bells to cease, and so there was silence. A great debt of gratitude is due to the head of the Roman Catholic Church for his courageous and generously minded act, and also for the splendid lead he has given his people at this time in all patriotic service. Not the least of Scotland's gifts to Malta has been its archbishop.

But it is of the hospitals I wish to speak, where so many wounded are finding a temporary home. Malta has assumed the rôle of nurse, and her breakwaters seem like arms stretched out to receive her burden of

Malta Hospitals

suffering. Once the hospital ship has passed within their shelter the rolling ceases, and the wounded feel that they have reached a haven of rest.

Quietly big barges come alongside, and almost tenderly the steam cranes lower the stretchers, swinging them gently into their places. Thus they are brought ashore. Valletta hospital is the one that is nearest and most easily reached, and it is being made a sorting base. It is one of the old buildings in the town, and has been a hospital for generations. Low-lying, one might at first think it unsuitable as a health resort. Yet once inside its thick, ancient walls, and you feel as if you had passed beyond the reach of the sun. The very solidness of the old masonry acts like a refrigerator, and within there is coolness.

Here is said to be one of the biggest wards in the world, with its two hundred beds, and it is a touching sight to look down its great length and see every cot occupied. Here are many of the dangerous cases which it would be unwise to move farther.

Malta Hospitals

Nurses, orderlies, Boy Scouts move quietly about. The latter are employed to run any odd errands for the men, to post their letters, and bring them magazines. Very useful and smart these Maltese lads are. A big courtyard affords a shady lounge for the convalescent, and once a week a concert is held there. A well staffed, thoroughly equipped hospital is the verdict of the visitor. Worthy of its ancient pedigree, it still ministers to the wounded as in the days of the old knights.

FULL OF ROYAL SCOTS

Across the harbour on a height which the breezes fan stands the hospital of Cottonera. It is not too big, and its awning-shaded verandahs are full just now with men of two battalions of the Royal Scots If an interesting view is a tonic the inmates do not lack that stimulus. There are some trees in the foreground, and the touch of green in the constant glare of white sand and stone is soothing to the eye. Beyond, the town slopes down to one of the numerous bays that open out into the grand harbour. Skimming its surface like flies are the restless dghaisas, which flit from shore to shore, or swarm round some newly-arrived liner. Across on the farther shore are tiers of white buildings too dazzling to look at, where Valletta climbs its rocky heights, that are topped by ancient stone bastions. It is all very picturesque, and the view must often cause the wounded men to forget their own suffering.

NAVAL DIGNITY

Across another creek or bay from Cottonera, proudly isolated on its own peninsula is Bighi Hospital. There is a seclusiveness about its position in keeping with its character. It is naval, and is conscious of all the dignity that belongs to the first service. It has more to recommend it than dignity, and any visitor would give it a first place amongst the Malta hospitals. There is a roominess about it that suits the man accustomed to the broad seas. Besides, it stands on a promontory that

Malta Hospitals

catches the first breezes from the Mediterranean. Fortunate is the patient who finds himself domiciled here. From Deputy-Surgeon-General Lawrence Smith down to the latest arrived nurse there is the consciousness of great traditions that have to be maintained, and the frank kindliness of the deck is repeated in the ward, as is also the discipline.

We recross back to Valletta and its heat, and visit now Floriana Hospital that gets the sun. You cannot reach it without having first to run the gauntlet of sunstroke, for somehow the sun seems to have the range of this blistering spot, and perhaps that is why it has earned so flowery a name!

Here are huge blocks of buildings. Once inside you forget, of course, their external monotony of design, and you are not tempted to look out except through coloured glasses. Yet here the work of healing goes steadily on, and men fight flies instead of Turks.

Floriana has this advantage, however,

Malta Hospitals

that when the men begin to move about they are at the centre of things. The recreation halls opened for their benefit in the town are at their door, and so as convalescents they have a better time than others.

Two miles farther out the hot dusty car track is Hamrun Hospital, an inspection of which is well worth the annoyance of getting there. It must be a delight to a doctor's heart. It recalls to mind the story of a bride. She was being congratulated by her friends, and they all used the same adjective about her husband calling him a model man. In her curiosity to learn the exact meaning of the word she consulted a dictionary and discovered that model was a " small imitation of the real article."

THE GROPING HAND

Hamrun is small, but a model. Of course, it is quite new, and, therefore, might be expected to have all the latest improvements. It exhales an atmosphere of up-to-dateness. Here all eye cases are being sent. In one of its wards I witnessed a pathetic scene. As I passed along I saw a hand groping above the blankets. It belonged to a patient whose eyes were shaded. I guessed its meaning. It was feeling for sympathy. The man was suffering, and he craved for the human touch. I put out my hand, and in a moment his closed round it and in the tremulous pulsebeat I read a telepathic message of comfort and relief. He was blind, and for the time speechless, all communication from the outside world was therefore by touch, and somehow in the short time I held his hand I felt that we were able to say quite a lot to each other, perhaps more to the point than if the thoughts had been put into words. I think he knew I was a chaplain, and that I was trying to convey the great truth, " The Eternal God is my refuge and underneath are the everlasting arms."

Come now to the largest hospital on the island. We descend first of all to the bowels of the earth by a sloping tunnel, and

Malta Hospitals

there we find a train waiting. With much puffing and waste of coal dust we emerge at last into the open, and get a view of Malta country life in the patches of land that are still unbuilt. It is like a congested Palestine. These little fields are all walled in, and have their watch tower to guard against thieves. Truly, a country like an individual carries its character in its face! Here, too, we see the Biblical methods of threshing, the oxen treading out the corn, and the Maltese unwillingness to accept its spirit, for the animals are all muzzled! We pass the old town of Citta Vecchia, which invites inspection and makes a good living on its historic past. But as it is not a guide-book I am writing, we will turn a deaf ear to the importunities of the army of guides on the platform who extol the wonders of catacomb and church. Another tunnel, and we have completed our eight miles by rail and reached the terminus, and see on a height before us block upon block of newly-built buildings. This is Imtarfa Hospital, the largest on the island.

THE SCOTTISH CLUB FOR SOLDIERS, VALLETTA.

Photo by Christien & Co., Malta.

Malta Hospitals

The older part was originally barracks, now it has been greatly added to, and we have an array of wards capable of holding 1,200 patients. Its isolation and its elevation have determined its scope. Thither are being sent infectious diseases and enteric cases. A glance at the mosquito netted beds tells its own tale, for flies are quick to diagnose certain fevers, and try to get a chance of digging into the hot skin and carrying away the infection to inject into some healthy victim.

WHEN THE CRUTCHES ARE DISCARDED

It is a far cry from here to St. Andrew's Hospital, which is second in size. Our best way is to face the engine soot again and take the train back to Valletta, and cross in one of the ferry boats to Sliema, and drive from there along a hilly road for about three miles. It is crowded just now with men in khaki. They get the princely allowance of 2s. a week, and therefore cannot afford to hire a carozze unless they club together, which they often do. But they are experiencing a new-found pleasure in the use of their limbs. For a man who did not know whether he would ever be able to walk again, and has had a taste of crutches, even a trudge in the heat has indescribable attractions. To feel that his limbs are all there and working is worth perspiring for. These are the men who have reached the last stage of their several flittings in Malta, and are now at the Convalescent Camp, just above St. Andrew's, christened by the Governor the other day "All Saints." Their next move will be the Dardanelles once more, and we will be kind enough to wish that we may never see them back again in Malta!

We have not time to stop at St. George's Hospital, which we pass on the way, and which has the distinction or disqualification of being worked without women. The first time I passed through its wards I felt that there was something lacking. The men of the R.A.M.C. may know their business, and make excellent nurses, but there is truth in

Malta Hospitals

the complaint one of the wounded made to my wife in a confidential moment.

"NO ONE TO TUCK YOU IN"

" There is no one to tuck you in and say good-night," he remarked wistfully.

I think St. George's must hold out no longer, but haul down the benedict flag, and welcome the sisters. Since writing the above this has been done.

St. Andrew's also stands on a hill, and has a magnificent set of buildings. If it is smaller than Imtarfa it can only be by a few beds, and it excels in its imposing architecture.

In this hospital there is one accomplished little nurse to whom I have quite lost my heart. Do not say it is shocking until you hear the end of the tale. There is always an end to everything, and sometimes very different from the beginning. So one should reserve judgment. I am sure if you could see her you would all admire her just as much as I do, especially the boys

Malta Hospitals

and girls. She is very perky—yes, that is the right adjective—and a great favourite with the men, though with the cooler weather her duties will not be so urgent. I must confess that when I discovered her I found reasons for going back to visit her hospital more than some others. She is doing her bit, only she spells it with an added " e," and the men all try to woo her to their bedside. She cocks her little head and looks at them so wisely, though I must admit there is a little cupboard love in her attentions, and she has an eye for something else—something that is a nuisance to them and a delight to her. She perches herself on the edge of the bed, then hops on to the patient's arm, and there is a fly less to bother. There, I have given my secret away. She is a little bird called the fly-catcher, and right zealously does she do her bite.

But even these great hospitals have overflowed their limits. To the back long rows of wooden huts have quickly risen. In fact they look like a little village, in

Malta Hospitals

America they would certainly be dignified with the title of town, if not of city. They bear the appropriate name of the apostle who was the pioneer in Malta of the healing art, St. Paul. His shadow is cast everywhere in this island, but surely nowhere does it fall with greater fitness than in the wards where men and women try to undo with skill and tenderness the havoc of the battle-field.

Farther up, cresting the height with its snowy canvas, is St. David's camp. The big marquee erected by the Guild of the United Free Church of Scotland towers in the centre like a mediaeval castle above the clustering roofs of the town it shelters. Here the fresh air cure is united with the art of the surgeon, for a breeze seems always to fan these streets of tents, and when Valletta is in liquidation with the heat St. David's has still to its credit a breath of air!

Now we will return, for All Saints' Camp does not concern us at present. It is not a hospital. At Spinola we stop. We enter

Malta Hospitals

its scattered encampment with some hesitancy, for it has changed its character so often that we are in doubt whether to reckon it a hospital or not. But if we have arrived at the right time, we will find many of its tents filled, not merely with the men who have been cured and who are waiting to rejoin their regiments, but with others just beginning the process.

If I were giving a prize for the most artistically laid out camps I would make a short leet of St. Patrick's and St. David's, and then toss up for the choice. I have seen both emerge from their swaddling clothes of mud, and blossom into gardens with their tents dotted amongst the rich bloom of flowers, and it has seemed like one of the conjuring tricks of the East. Here the Y.M.C.A., which has done so much for Malta under the superintendence of Mr. Wheeler, has erected a large wooden hall, and men can listen there to concert or lecture without being disturbed by the flapping of canvas.

But we must hurry on, if we are to have

Malta Hospitals

even a bird's-eye view of the scenes round which are woven the stories of these pages. St. John's hospital is an imposing building. It was the newest school in Sliema, and one envies the children who will have such delightful classrooms. I asked our chaplain there, the Rev. William Cowan, what was distinctive about it, and he replied the desire on the part of its patients to come back to it again. That certainly is a good certificate of character for any hospital, though I do not think that it is the only one in Malta that has earned this compliment.

We have scarcely time to do more than look in at the little hospital of St. Ignatius, which is hidden away in the suburbs of Sliema. To pass into its cool corridors on a burning day is refreshing for the visitor, and what must it be for the patient! The wards here with their old-fashioned thick walls have managed to shut out the sun, and in Malta the most highly appreciated blessing is shade. Someone has likened life here in summer to sitting on a red-hot

Malta Hospitals

brick, that is gradually getting hotter. So you can imagine that the cool spots are little heavens, and St. Ignatius is one of them. Perhaps its patients may not agree with me, but then they do not know what the other hospitals are like, and it is only by contrast that you can judge.

OUTWITTING THE GUARD

Forrest Hospital stands on a hill, and its discipline is pretty strict. One day an Australian patient, to whom a rule was like a red rag, determined to go out without permission, but naturally he was stopped by the guard at the gate. He was not to be baulked, and he said so ; but the guard only smiled. However, he laughs best who laughs last. The Colonial got twenty others of his fellow-countrymen to "bunch" as they call it and to make a rush through the open gate. It was only a lark and they wheeled round and came back, but not the whole twenty ; one had slipped away unobserved, the instigator of the plot !

Malta Hospitals

Next we come to Tigne. Its base is sea-washed, and the breezes burdened with the brine ought to be a tonic to its inmates. Its high blocks almost depress with their monotony, and when you know that they are full to overflowing with suffering humanity, the heart of the visitor sinks. Manoel is a little world by itself. On a jutting peninsula, with only a bridge as a neck, it is cut off from the rest of the island. Isolation determines its character, for here one finds many infectious cases.

I have not yet spoken of St. Elmo or Baviere Hospitals; both have the attraction of an interesting seascape. In the former is a soldier who has to undergo to-day his eighteenth operation. He was quite cheery last night, and spoke of the operating theatre as a matter of course. One can get accustomed to almost anything!

Now I have reached the limits of my chapter before I have got to the end of my story; but I have tried to give you a passing snapshot of the principal hospitals of the island, and in so far as they have

Malta Hospitals

distinctive characteristics to emphasise such. May you never test the accuracy of my sketch by experience. If you do, you will say that half has not been told of the comfort and the kindness enjoyed by our wounded in the Malta Hospitals.

The Blue Sisters' Hospital must not be forgotten. Of it many an officer has grateful memories. From its balcony a magnificent panorama stretched itself of distant town, and sun-lit waters, and stone-fenced fields. Through its cool corridors the Sisters were ever flitting in their picturesque garb with noiseless steps on their errand of mercy.

In a word one might sum up the general scheme that governed the arrangements of the hospitals in Malta.

First there were those of which I have spoken in this chapter. These were for the more serious cases. Then there were the Hospital Camps, a new feature, which I think had never been tried before, where the patients were housed under canvas instead of in a building. These have

Malta Hospitals

proved most successful. Next were the Convalescent Camps, of which I will speak more fully later. To one of these the recovering patient was sent on quitting hospital. Last of all was the Concentration Camp, or stepping-off place. Here the man who had passed through the other stages was once more in full regimentals, and awaited a ship to take him back to the front.

CHAPTER III

A SAD MARCH PAST

IT is not from the saluting flag that I am going to ask you to view the march past of our brave soldiers, but from the hospital ward. They come in an endless procession, halt maybe for days or weeks, and then pass out. Some go to rejoin the colours, and step out again briskly to the sound of the drum; some with a smile on their wan faces go home; others are carried out to their " long home." Under the shady trees of Pieta there are many new-made graves, and the chaplain stops on his return from another funeral beside a little plot and thinks of a boyish face that had looked up at his so wistfully and frankly from the pillow.

" He was a brave lad," he murmurs to

A Sad March Past

himself; "and it did me good to know him."

That face is looking into some other heart far away, and its smile brings a sweet ache, and the longing to see the lonely grave at which the unknown chaplain is the only mourner.

THE BEGINNING OF THE PROCESSION

The march past first comes into view at the harbour mouth. Heaving slightly on the swell outside is a stately ship, with a big red cross painted on her side.

As she passes into the still waters behind the breakwater the wearied sufferers on board feel a soothing stillness. The engines have stopped, and the swinging has ceased. There is no noisy bustle about the arrival of this ship, even the crowds of dghaisas keep away. Then quietly great barges move alongside, cranes creak, and a strange burden rises from the deck of the ship, is swung over the side, and lowered into the waiting barge. It is a stretcher with a motionless

A Sad March Past

form upon it. From under the light covering two feet are visible at one end, and a head, possibly bandaged, at the other. Never did the arm of steel handle its burden more gently. A mother's hands could not lay her babe to rest in its cradle more tenderly than does the unconscious crane place its living weight in the closely packed line of stretchers on the barge's deck. Then comes the journey ashore. Rows of ambulance waggons are waiting, but the Malta streets were not made for wounded, and many a sharp pang there must be ere the shelter of the cool hospital ward is reached.

"It was like heaven to get here," murmured one wounded man to me. Some sleep actually for days after their arrival, and "Nature's sweet restorer" is their best nurse.

How quickly the wards fill up: For the usual salutation at breakfast is, "I see there is another ship in to-day from the Dardanelles."

Its passengers have now become the chaplain's parishioners.

A Sad March Past

PARISHIONERS

As the chaplain comes quietly along the rows of beds to see the new arrivals he is impressed with the stillness of the ward, a cooling peace pervades it. There is suffering, but it is scarcely articulate. How brave our heroes are! If all Britain's sons are of the same stuff we are unconquerable.

Thanks to the generosity of Greenock friends, and the kindness of the *Greenock Telegraph*, both Mr. Campbell and myself are supplied with a welcome gift for each sufferer; something that will enable him to withdraw his thoughts from his pain in the shape of interesting magazines or papers. Until they came there was a dearth of anything to read, especially in the hospitals outside Valletta.

The coming of them perhaps deserves a notice. Having seen with my own eyes the growing heap on the floor of the *Telegraph* Office before I left Greenock, I was able to reassure my friends that the pro-

A Sad March Past

mised help would be ample when it would arrive; but in Malta at present that is a matter of great uncertainty. Letters come in weeks late, and one may be glad to get them then. The great art of officialdom is to hand an importunate enquirer on to somebody else. It reminds me of a card game I used to play called " The Old Maid." The successful player was the one who could best pass on to his neighbour the fatal card.

At last we got word that in some part of the naval dockyard there were parcels which were not munitions. We hired a conveyance and started off in pursuit. A casual street accident revealed the Gaelic minister in a new light, as I saw him holding down the head of a horse which had fallen. I managed to get a wound in my thumb, which made my friend remark that he did not know I had such a lot of good blood in my veins before. In this climate wounds bleed profusely. A handy ambulance man tied me up, and we were off again in search of the Greenock bundles. We might not have

A Sad March Past

found them had it not been for a lucky encounter which verified the text, "Cast thy bread upon the waters and it will return unto thee after many days." In one of the offices we entered was a corporal who had tasted of our teapot, and at once he put himself and everybody else about to get on the right trail. At last, after another drive, we reached a store-room, and there our hearts were delighted to see facing us bundle upon bundle of well-packed literature. It took six men to carry them to our conveyance, and though we paid our man two and a half times more than we had bargained with him for, he left us with a last reproachful look at the pile of parcels. The fact that it was mostly "light" literature did not affect its weight!

However, now, thanks to Greenock generosity, we are well equipped for our work, and we never start our visiting without taking a large bag well packed with magazines and Testaments. The latter are always welcomed, for most of the wounded have lost theirs, and the men who have

A Sad March Past

faced death and barely escaped from it have a hunger for "The Word of Life."

HUMOUR IN THE WARD

Occasionally the sad work is lightened by a ray of humour. Mr. Campbell, going through one of his hospitals recently, came on a man who seemed to be suffering severely.

"Can I do anything for you?" he asked in a sympathetic voice as he bent over him.

"There is one thing I would like," answered the soldier.

"What is that?" was the ready answer.

"I wonder if you could tell me where I could get an orange?"

"Oh," interrupted the generous-hearted chaplain, "leave that to me, I will find some for you."

As he left he did not notice the look of mystification on the man's face. Now, the orange season is past in Malta, and though a few months ago there was a super-

A Sad March Past

abundance of them, at present it is the most difficult of fruits to obtain. However, difficulty seems to add zest to my colleague, and certainly he never spares himself. There was a lady at whose house he had been in the country, and he had seen her orange groves—and remembered. To her he hastened with his story of the poor soldier who was suffering, and who had taken such a craving for an orange. Most kindly she sent to her gardens to have her trees searched for the last orange of summer. There was more than one discovered, and Mr. Campbell returned next day to the hospital with a parcel of generous dimensions, and a glad heart. He had secured "the water from the well of Bethlehem," not without effort, and he was anticipating the glad look of joy on the orange-hungry man's face.

When he reached his bedside he was surprised at another kind of look, and all the lame and limp in the ward had gathered within earshot at Mr. Campbell's approach. There was unmistakably a smile lurking

A Sad March Past

about their mouths, which might do them as much good as oranges.

"Here they are," said the chaplain enthusiastically as he laid his burden on the bed.

"Did you not get my letter?" asked the wounded soldier.

"No," was the surprised reply. Evidently there was something that needed an explanation.

"I wrote you immediately after you left. I saw afterwards that you had misunderstood my meaning," remarked the sufferer.

It was now the chaplain's turn to look mystified.

"Your letter has not reached me yet," he said.

Meanwhile the oranges were lying neglected. It seemed as if the Bible story of the dearly secured water, which was unused, was going to be repeated.

"What I wished to ask for," said the man with a smile, "was not oranges, but an Orange Lodge."

A Sad March Past

At this there was a general ripple of laughter.

"Well, perhaps these oranges may do you more good, and be less exciting," responded the chaplain, as he handed over the fruit to be enjoyed along with the joke.

Here is another story which I hope all Presbyterians will live up to, and I trust other denominations will pardon.

I was going my rounds, and in one ward I asked,

"Are there any Presbyterians here?"

"Yes," came the answer from a bed. "The man opposite me is one." As he spoke the wounded soldier pointed to a vacant cot. Its occupant was evidently out.

I went over and read the name on the card.

"You are mistaken," I answered, "this is a C.O.E. man."

"Well, I thought he was a Presbyterian, because he is always reading his Bible."

A Sad March Past

THE CRUTCH WALK

I call it this, for it describes the third stage in the march past. Now we see the men who are becoming convalescent. They can get beyond the ward, some on the arms of their companions, some on their own feet, and some on crutches. When they get the length of the streets where are they to go? This is a most important question, for temptation lurks at every corner, and somehow at the most critical point the military authorities seem to think that their special care terminates, except for certain orders, which, alas, are too easily evaded.

The need was so urgent that Mr. Campbell and I felt that something must be done. Of course the people in Malta are very kind to the wounded. They are given theatre entertainments, and sometimes garden parties, but what the poor fellows need to keep them straight is a home and a kindly Christian atmosphere.

So we got our hall, and had it opened with a tea. Mrs. Mackinnon takes charge of

A Sad March Past

this, and it occupies her whole time. In the forenoon she is busy preparing cool drinks—lemon squash—which are given gratis to the thirsty men, for everyone has a thirst here. At 2 p.m. the hall is opened, and from then until 7 p.m. there is a constant stream in and out of the halt and lame. Already the tables are loaded with the magazines and papers sent from Greenock. We have provided writing material and many a mother's heart at home will be gladdened because her son found the cool hall with its ink and pens. Also there is a piano, and it is wonderful how musical the soldiers are. Tea is served free to all, and fifty loaves a day are sliced and spread with butter and jam and given to our wounded without charge. But I shall refer more fully to this club in a subsequent chapter.

THE OUTWARD BOUND

Crutches have now been flung aside, and we hear the brisk beat of a drum. A

A Sad March Past

column of men in khaki is leaving for the front. Malta has done its work and left pleasant memories. We follow them to the harbour, and witness another March Past that thrills us with pride. Transport after transport, laden with troops, rest for a few hours in the shelter of these waters and then move on towards the sound of the guns.

Let us pause on the Barracca, and look down on this other empire of Britain, her domain of the sea. Perhaps nowhere is it seen to better advantage. I do not mean the mere waste of waters, for from deck and headland their defiant strength, which human brain and muscle have curbed, may be viewed with far grander effect; but I speak of a world of greater interest, which has its home on the deep—a race of men liveried in woollen jersey, oil-skin, brass buttons, and gilded braid.

There in the centre of the harbour swings at anchor an ugly, dull-coloured mass of floating steel. It is a British cruiser. Her three short, black funnels,

A Sad March Past

the bores of her long guns pointing fore and aft, make a sombre silhouette against the glittering sea. Like a stinging reptile of the ocean, she crouches in the waves; or rather, like a coffin, in a garden of flowers, she jars on the senses. Death, cruel, horrid, is suggested by her dusky sides, save for one mast with its cross-spar. Yet, to-day, there is a human touch about her; grotesque it may be, but welcome, if not to the eye, at least to the heart—she has her washing out: Ribbon lines of white relieve the sternness of her bows.

Gliding out into the blaze of sunshine is a sight that rouses within one the spirit of one's ancestors. The tall, tapering masts of a full-rigged ship make a stately outline against the sky; from a network of ropes and tackle her yards stretch gracefully out until, as silently, majestically she moves outward behind the puffing tug, you instinctively call her "Queen of the Sea." Like a phantom of the past she flits noiselessly amidst that scene of belching funnels

A Sad March Past

and churning screws, and you appreciate the poetic as well as the heroic touch in the time-worn title, " The wooden walls of Old England."

But the harbour invites a closer inspection.

A chaplain's work is full of variety and opportunity if he is quick to seize it. As an illustration of this let me give you a glimpse of the last two days, and you will see how it was the unexpected opportunity that was the most fruitful of interest and results.

Mr. Campbell and myself started in the morning in our dghaisa to visit a fortress and hospital some distance away. As we crossed the harbour my friend's quick eye detected the presence of a new steamer lying at anchor, the *Baron Ardrossan.*

"Let us see if there are any Scots on board," remarked my indefatigable companion.

We turned our boat in and alongside. Red-tape demands passes for almost everything here, and certainly for boarding a

A Sad March Past

Government ship. But those who know Mr. Campbell will agree that he carries his certificate in his open kindly face, and when that is united with a strong will, it will be readily understood that the officer at the deck end of the rope ladder yielded to our sudden assault. Mr. Campbell's heart was delighted when he heard that there were eighteen Gaelic-speaking sailors on board. They were at a meal in the fo'c'sle at that moment, and thither we went in a blazing heat that made the iron deck seem like burning coals under our soles.

I never saw such a look of astonishment on men's faces before as when we put our heads into the close mess-room. But it was intensified when Mr. Campbell uttered some magic words in Gaelic. The knives and forks literally dropped out of the crew's hands in their amazement, and I saw a wondering smile break over their bearded and begrimed faces.

Of course I could only be a spectator, but I saw that my friend held them from the start. What he was saying I did not

A Sad March Past

understand, only at intervals I saw them lift their hands in answer to some question. We always carry some literature with us, for which we are most grateful to our Greenock friends and others. The ship was sailing at 4 p.m., but we promised to be back again at 3 p.m. and hold a service.

About our real errand that day, which has become side-issued in this story, and about the stirring tales told us by the men fresh from the blood-stained fields of the Dardanelles I must speak again. It was the unexpected incident that left on us the deepest impression.

After lunch, accompanied by Mrs. Mackinnon, the three of us set out. Again we boarded the *Baron Ardrossan* and were received most courteously by the captain and chief officer. Seats were arranged on the bridge deck, and the Highlanders were called there. A deck chair was provided for Mrs. Mackinnon, and the service began. I have been at many impressive religious meetings, but few have equalled this in uniqueness of feeling. The very strange-

A Sad March Past

ness of it appealed to the men themselves. They never had had a religious service before on board. All around sounded the creaking of cranes and the puffing of donkey engines with the confused noises of a ship preparing to get under way. Suddenly the unaccustomed strain in such a place began to penetrate the din and rise above it. It was the melody of a Gaelic psalm to the tune of Kilmarnock. I saw the "Sassenachs" on the deck stop in their work and look up in amazement, and well they might, as they listened to those eighteen men singing praise to God. A very rough looking lot a casual spectator might say. They had just been summoned from their work and came as they were. Some were barefooted, all were perspiring and begrimed; but to Him who searcheth the heart there must have been something heavenly in that song, that wafted its message of faith from the very midst of death-dealing explosives.

Then came the prayer. I noticed that most of the men stood during it, betokening

A Sad March Past

the land from which they came. They were from Lewis. It seemed to me that as the pastor led those men near to God in their mother tongue a hush crept over the ship. Certainly the hoarse shouting and coarse words appeared to lessen. Somehow men felt that God was being worshipped there. The minister told me the text of his address afterwards. It dealt with the sheepfold and the Gate. I saw its impression in the glistening of more than one eye and the moistening of more than one cheek.

The captain and chief officer showed us every kindness. Perhaps the secret of it was in the way the commander spoke of his men.

"They are a splendid set of good living fellows," he said, and maybe that was why even at a busy moment he was willing to let them have that short time of spiritual strengthening.

On reaching home that evening another surprise awaited us. Our own boys, as we call the Greenock lads of the Argyll and

A Sad March Past

Sutherland Highlanders, had arrived on a transport on their way to the Dardanelles. Some of the officers dined with us that night at our hotel, and next morning Mr. Campbell and I set out to visit the men.

There was a large number from our own congregations, as well as from the other churches in Greenock. What hearty handshaking we had as we recognised the familiar faces under the unfamiliar helmets. Friends at home had not sent us away with an empty purse, and we thought that this was an occasion for emptying it a little. So we invested in chocolate and cigarettes until the errand boy who took our parcels to the boat could not comfortably carry any more. Greenock was reaching out her hands through us in farewell to her brave sons.

We held a service for the men in their mess-room, and I gave a short address, and were it not for the unfamiliar surroundings I might have thought myself at home as I looked into the faces of my own members. It was difficult to tear ourselves away, and

A Sad March Past

our hearts went with the brave lads whom we would fain have accompanied if chaplain's committees would only take into account personal ties.

We could not wait to see them sail, as duties summoned us to a hospital eight miles distant, but Mrs. Mackinnon kept vigil by the harbour, and waved them an adieu from the "old friends at home" as later in the afternoon they steamed out to the unknown.

The work here was the zest of ready results. Just before I came there was a week of interesting meetings, in which Mr. Campbell and Mr. Sim took a leading part, assisted by some of the Anglican chaplains. At the week-night services in one of the hospitals there were almost a hundred men present, and fifty-one professed a change of life. Facing death has brought eternal realities near, and never have I seen men more eager for the preaching of the Gospel or the reception of Christian literature. Many are here to-day and within the week may be dead on the field of battle.

ST. PAUL'S HOSPITAL CAMP, MALTA.

A Sad March Past

THE FAREWELL

It has its bright and its sad side. One day on going into a ward you meet a specially cheery face.

"I am going home to-morrow, sir," says the lad, who cannot hide his joy. "There is a hospital ship in, and I am to be sent with it."

He is the envied of all. "Going home." How sweetly the words sound! They have a sad echo, however. There is another "going home," when for the last time the brave soldier follows the drum, only now it is muffled. This at first is one of the hardest duties of a chaplain, and I will confess my eyes dimmed with tears as I committed my first coffin to a soldier's grave. It was that of a young officer, Lieutenant Leggat of the 7th Scottish Rifles. The hour was sunset, and I stood robed at the cemetery gate.

Nearer and nearer came the sound of muffled drums. Five coffins were borne in that last march to the "long home."

A Sad March Past

There were two officers and three privates. The former had each a separate grave.

Slowly, reverently were the bodies lifted from the gun carriages. In this land of ceremony even the Presbyterian burial adds a little to its stern simplicity, and I walked before the coffin reading passages of Scripture, until we reached the grave. Two brother officers and one private stood beside me as the mourners. Then, when all was over, the firing party awakened the evening stillness with their solemn shots. Silence followed for a moment, then on a silver trumpet rang out the notes of "The Last Post," and to the fancy they seemed to blend with the blast of the angel trumpet which will awake the sleeper from the tomb.

At the close I thought I was alone, for I stood looking into the grave trying to do for the unknown sorrowing hearts at home the sad service they were denied. Suddenly my reverie was interrupted; the private had spoken. He too was left alone beside me, and his voice shook with emotion.

A Sad March Past

" He was my officer," was all he could say.

Yet what a testimony to the British Army, what an assurance of victory in these words.

Perhaps I can best close this chapter by quoting the lines written by one of our chaplains here, the Rev. William Cowan of Banchory, which he entitles:

A MILITARY FUNERAL

With sound of plaintive brass, and deep-toned drum,
   And Britain's banner for a funeral pall,
   And measured tread of men whose footsteps fall
In time with that sad minstrelsy, they come
And carry to its narrow earthly home
   The coffin'd clay of one they late did call
   Comrade or friend, nor deemed of him that all
Could lie beneath that empty helmet's dome.
Beside the grave with arms reversed they stand,
   While prayers are offered, motionless until,
Obedient to the word of sharp command,
   They wake the echoes from the distant hill
With well-timed volleys; then the bugle band
   Sounds forth its call to rest, and all is still.

CHAPTER IV

THE LAND OF THE OPEN HAND

TO whom this title refers I will leave you for a little to guess. The Australian and New Zealand wounded I am sure think it suitable, and they are shrewd fellows; and I know it is the name which unconsciously the country suggested is earning out here.

Now, if you have an hour to spare this afternoon, you could not do better than spend it with me at our Soldiers' Club, or shall I more truly call it our " Greenock Tea Room," in Valletta, and thus give half of my secret away.

Before we turn into Strada Forni we hear the sound of a soldiers' chorus borne up the street, and we know things are in full swing, and we can guess which chaplain has

The Land of the Open Hand

dropped in to give " go " to the afternoon's entertainment.

With such an advertisement flung far and wide, and the sniff of delicious tea on a nearer approach, no wonder we encounter a queue at the doors. I have brought you at three o'clock, the busiest hour, and we need to push our way through the men that crowd the short flight of stairs and little lobby, waiting for vacant seats inside.

On entering we see that our guess as to the chaplain was correct. There are really two present. Near the piano stands Rev. Robert Menzies, and his Camphill congregation should see him now, for he is at his best. With pipe in one hand, with which he beats time, he is singing with great feeling and expression a favourite song of the soldiers. Almost unconsciously he has broken into it, as is his way, and the men have picked up the chorus, and Rev. C. McEchern, of Tighnabruaich, one of our other chaplains, with his usual alertness, has seated himself at the piano and picked up the air on its keys, and the whole

The Land of the Open Hand

thing is going with a mighty swing as we enter.

The men are mostly in blue coats, the class we want. They have not actually reached the convalescent stage yet, and have to be back to their hospitals by six o'clock. Their pay is two shillings a week, so I do not think our Greenock friends will grudge their gift of a cup of tea to those who have suffered, even to the sacrifice of limbs, for their sake, and who have not the money in hand to pay for such a luxury. Some day the authorities will acknowledge that Greenock, as well as the doctors and nurses, has done its part in helping to cure our wounded. Already the men have made this acknowledgment in multitudes. Your ears would tingle if you heard how they attributed their quicker recovery to the marvellous effects of the Greenock teas.

Let us peep into the kitchen for a moment. It is a busy scene, and there is no space for idle spectators. In fact, it is like a kitchen on one of our Pullman cars, where every inch of space has had to be made

The Land of the Open Hand

use of. Here there have been great alterations, everything that is not of immediate use has been cleared out. Shelves have been erected. These are piled with plates of bread that are eloquent of the forenoon toil of the ladies. Fifty loaves have been cut into slices and spread with butter and jam. We can afford no other luxury than this now, the days of cakes and buns are gone. Then there were about sixty or seventy to provide for, now there are between four hundred and five hundred daily.

Yet the cruse of oil fails not. Yesterday I got copies of *The Christchurch Press*, New Zealand, and *The Auckland Herald*, in which my articles had appeared, and with them a cheque for twenty pounds to swell the funds. Glasgow, through the energy of Mr. Menzies, is responding, and Scotland is winning a name for openness of heart and generosity, which will be carried by these thousands of Colonials back to their homelands ; and in the days to come when they refight their battles over again, and tell of their wounds, I know they will not

The Land of the Open Hand

forget to mention Greenock in grateful tones, and they will always think of Scotland as the land of the open hand. I have chosen that phrase as a title, for it worthily fits the town and country that have so generously spread the tables in this little island for worn warriors. In no other place in Malta is a free tea given to our soldiers daily, and people are wondering when it is going to stop. But it is not going to stop. Just now the expense, even for simple bread and butter and jam, with tea, approximates £2 a day.

Now, we are not wanted in the kitchen, so we had better move out. The ladies are too busy to talk. We catch a glimpse of the gas stoves with their kettles singing merrily, and turn back into the hall. Here there has also been a great transformation. We have refurnished it. A dozen little square tables with five or six chairs round each have taken the place of the cumbersome forms and trestle tables. At the end of the room a large table covered with green baize has been reserved for special

The Land of the Open Hand

papers and magazines, and another for writing.

THE OPENING OF THE HALL

While we glance round this busy scene let me tell you something about its start.

To understand hospital life in this sirocco-swept island one has to experience the humid grip of the hot air as it enwraps you like some invisible octopus, wrings every particle of vitality out of the body, and leaves you as limp as a sucked orange.

The men who have got the length of sitting on their beds or limping along the wards have nothing else to think of but the heat, and it is far from an invigorating subject. Therefore Mr. Campbell and I felt that we would be true trustees of the money entrusted to our charge if we got up a home for our brave lads.

I need not speak of initial difficulties. This is a land of inertia, and the only cold water that is to be found here is that which is thrown on new schemes. Authorities are

The Land of the Open Hand

conservative. However, difficulties are to my colleague as a red rag to a bull.

The day before the opening Mrs. Mackinnon met a group of wounded men outside the door of the hall. They had just come to see the place where the home was to be. Poor fellows! If only the friends at home could realise what this meant, they also would share in the pleasure they have been the means of giving to others.

Long before the hour streams of blue-jacketed men, some with arms in a sling, others on crutches, could be seen making their way to the hall, which had been cleaned and garnished, and smiled its welcome with the perfume and freshness of newly-cut flowers.

One man, who on the previous Sunday had hobbled a mile with only one boot on to attend Divine service, repeated the journey, and his happy face almost brought tears of joy to our eyes. Would any Greenock church-goer have the courage and determination to go a mile to church in his stocking-soles, if because of a wound he could not get his boot on?

The Land of the Open Hand

Every man who was invited, and who could come, was there. The little hall was full. It was Mrs. Mackinnon's province to look after the tea, and the white clothed tables were soon laden with tempting eatables, and the cup that cheers was never more relished.

"My! I wish we could take these ladies out to the Dardanelles to make us tea like that!" I overheard one soldier say to his friend as he laid down his cup.

There was reason to be proud, for the men manifested their relish of the treat in no doubtful fashion. On the platform, gracing the occasion, were also the two chief medical men in Malta, Colonel Sleman, principal medical officer, under whose charge are all the numerous hospitals, and Colonel Ballance, the famous brain specialist. The latter spoke with such effect that I feel I cannot do better than give you some of his sentences.

"Britain," he said, "is face to face with a foe who for many years has planned her destruction. It is necessary, therefore, that

The Land of the Open Hand

every individual should keep as fit physically and spiritually as possible. Sacrifice is the rule of all that is best in life. A titanic struggle such as Germany is waging at the present is only possible when the entire nation, heart and soul, is at the back of its leaders. This can only be brought about when they are dominated by one idea. Their philosophy, summed up in a word, is this: Strength is extolled as the only virtue; weakness is proclaimed to be a vice and deadly sin. The weak are declared to have no claim to protection. The dogmas of religion and morality are taught as having no binding force on the individual. Humanitarian ideals are laughed at as only a contemptible expression. The German is educated to believe that no laws or promises can bind the State, only its own will. In this war, therefore, there is a clash of two systems of thought. We are fighting not for material objects but for a spiritual ideal. When a quarrel is for money or for a strip of territory peace can be concluded without moral loss. To make peace when an ideal

The Land of the Open Hand

is at stake is to be false to the voices which tell us that man is born for other things than to enjoy the moral and material heritage of his fathers. This is why Britain cannot give up fighting, however great her losses, till victory is secured, for to do so would be treason to all mankind.

" There are three reasons which chiefly influence the conduct of a man in this world—personal interest, social duty, religious duty. For my part, I shall hold that the last is the only all-powerful influence. The fact of Christ is the great satisfying and purifying force in the world, both for the individual and the nation. To belong to the British Navy or Army to-day is to bear a part in the greatest struggle for right or truth that has ever been fought on this blood-stained earth. In this noble contest it is required of you to be pure in body as well as brave in spirit. If it is your lot never to return, you will leave an immortal work behind you in the liberation of mankind from a foul and grasping tyranny; you will have become one of the makers of a future

The Land of the Open Hand

rescued from the menace of vile ambitions and merciless cruelty. And if it is given to you to pass into the happier day and share the peace won by the true heart and unfaltering arm of your country, you will find such a satisfaction in the name of Briton as no man living has ever known."

Colonel Sleman, in a few words, spoke of the value of the work being done by all who at this time came out to assist the troops. It made little difference whether they were in Lemnos or Malta; what mattered was that they were giving their help.

The hero of the stocking foot, Lance-Corporal Taylor, Christchurch, New Zealand, moved a vote of thanks to the ladies.

Another cup of tea followed before the men parted. Teapots need to have no bottoms here, or at least the bottom must never be reached, for there is always a great thirst, and tea has come into its own as the most quenching drink.

But let us have a talk with some of the men, and get their stories at first hand.

The Land of the Open Hand

BURIED ALIVE

Here is one with all the skin on his face peeled off, and he is just out for the first day with his new face, which is extremely raw to look at. Very simply he tells us one of the most astounding tales ever narrated.

"It was like this," he said. "Some of us were talking in a trench, not thinking of any danger, when suddenly the Turks began to fire, and we heard the hurtling of a shell. The rest of the fellows at once made for a dug-out. I was last, and, of course, could not go faster than the man in front. With a bang the thing plopped right in beside us. I threw myself on my face, and in an instant there was a most terrific roar, and I felt tons of earth tumbling on top of me. I lost consciousness. After a while I recovered my senses. At first I could not think where I was. My surroundings seemed so strange, and I could not move. Then memory came back, and I recalled the shell bursting, and realised that I was buried alive. I gave

The Land of the Open Hand

myself up for lost. And I can tell you, Padre, I did some harder thinking in these moments than I ever did in my life before."

There is an earnestness in his voice as he says this, whose spiritual note our ears have become trained to detect. These men have struck the deeper foundations of life in those moments when the surface debris has been cleared aside by the grim reality of death.

"Then," he continues, "I thought another shell had burst on top of me. The earth began to choke me. How I managed to breathe so far was owing to the soil being lumped and air getting through. Now the crevices got choked. Then my ear detected a sound that gave me hope. My chums had set themselves to dig me out, and it was the loose earth from their spades that was smothering me, and their knocks that sounded like other shells bursting. I can tell you I was glad when I got the first real mouthful of air. I left most of the skin of my face behind me, but I was glad to get off in the end so cheaply. I am feeling all right now, and expect to be marked down for the convalescent camp in a few days."

TURKISH HUMOUR

"The Turks gave us a laugh one day," another man says as we sit down for a talk with him. "Our trenches were very close, and there was a good deal of bombing going on. At our particular part, however, things were very quiet, and some of us were having a smoke, when suddenly flop into our trench came something that made us jump. I tell you we were not long in clearing out from the spot. Most of us dived into dug-outs to await the explosion, but it did not come off. We waited for a while, and still the thing didn't burst. Then we came out and had a look at it, and found that it was an old tin can, just thrown over to give us a fright. We can see the joke of it now, though we did not at the time."

Thus we chat on, and between the sups of tea we catch glimpses of the battlefield. Amidst the hum of conversation battles are fought over again and notes compared.

The Land of the Open Hand

Here there are strange meetings, for the club is proving a valuable centre for all the men.

OUR HUNGRY BOYS

Now, just let us stand up and take a general look round. There is one thing that gives us pleasure, and that is the way the lads go for the bread and butter. I would almost add that there is a touch of pathos about it, for the boys are dreadfully hungry. Remember that many of them are just recovered from fevers or other illness, during which they were partially starved for medical reasons, and now they have a ravenous appetite. Many of them are boys after all, and just as between meals they might go to their mother for "a piece," so they come into this home, where the ladies are doing their best to mother them. Every mother who has a son of her own will know what this means, and I do not think she would have it in her heart to deny them their request. Perhaps the mothers at home will help us to hand these "pieces" to the hungry boys out here.

The Land of the Open Hand

Yesterday one of the chief medical men of the island, who is in command of a big hospital here, said he very heartily approved of our work. There were societies, he remarked, getting large sums of money at present from the public for purposes that could almost be dispensed with. For himself, he would only give to those who were in direct contact with the men, and especially to those who were trying to build them up physically. Such teas were a valuable help to the work of the hospitals.

To-day one Aberdonian said rather ruefully to Mrs. Mackinnon: "The doctor says I maun be fed up, but I havena seen the beginnin' o' it yet."

"Are you not feeling strong?" she asked.

"Na; I'm nearly as weak as the tea in the hospitals."

So the chaff goes on, and the men speak their mind, and feel at home.

HOME NEWS

But one of the chief attractions of the hall is home news. At one end we have

The Land of the Open Hand

had a large paper rack erected, containing about thirty fairly large pigeon holes. Into these the newspapers are sorted. Through the assistance of the *Greenock Telegraph* a letter asking for periodicals appeared in about sixty publications in Great Britain, and there has been an immediate and generous response. The Welshman or Irishman has only to go to his particular pigeon hole, and there he will doubtless find his local paper, and for the next half-hour, as he settles himself in his chair, he is oblivious of his surroundings. In one pigeon-hole are *Greenock Telegraphs*, in another *Glasgow Heralds*. On the row below may be found the *Sydney Morning Herald*, or the Melbourne *Argus*. I have not yet counted the variety of publications, but I should think that there would be over a hundred different kinds. The Rothesay man can find his *Buteman*, the Lovat Scout from Tobermory his *Oban Times*. Paisley is about the only town in Scotland unrepresented.

Mrs. Mackinnon has been ably assisted in this work by Miss Daisy Jenkin from the start, and several other ladies, who have plied the bread knife with unceasing vigour.

NATIONAL TYPES

The room affords a splendid opportunity for making a study of national character and temperament. Here, perhaps, as nowhere else in Malta, or indeed in the whole sphere of war, do the varied allies rub shoulders. We can only glance at these distinctions just now. They would make an article in themselves.

Very prominent is the Australian. He is a big fellow, and has a free and easy manner and masterful stride. There is something invitingly frank and breezy about him, and there is little self-consciousness.

"I say, Padre," said one of them yesterday, in a voice that the whole room might hear if it liked, "I want your opinion on the immortality of the soul."

The question was very characteristic. These men speak quite freely of the deeper truths of religion in a way that astonishes the Scot. Of course, they are also perfectly frank about subjects of the very opposite kind.

The Land of the Open Hand

The New Zealander is a blending of the Scot and Australian. He is quieter in his talk and his Colonial accent is not quite so pronounced.

There are Indians here, too, our dusky allies. How they found out our room I do not know, but they got a kindly welcome and a cup of tea, and they showed their white teeth in a smile of appreciation. Tall, dignified, quiet men, who insist before leaving on going to the kitchen door and salaaming most graciously to the ladies. Frenchmen, too, have found their way here, and they seemed delighted when one of the ladies carried on a brisk conversation with them.

There is the Lovat Scout, with the stride of the gamekeeper ; the strapping Scottish Horse man, the Englishman of varied county and accent, the Welshman and Irish, the Newfoundlander, the thoughtful Edinburgh boy, and the innocent looking laddie of the West. Here they all are in a small hall, finding speech more easy because of the tea, and joining in the same swelling chorus that proclaims the unity and spirit of the British Empire.

CHAPTER V

MALTA RAINBOWS

"BLAME the sirocco."

It is our scapegoat in Malta. If a man has a pain in his head or his leg, or if he loses his temper, it is because of this ill-favoured wind, that blows from the south to the south-east and carries an unwelcome whiff of the African deserts with it.

Weeks have gone past and I have not sent you a letter. Well, it is our old enemy the sirocco that is to blame. Not that personally I have suffered much from this moist and sticky hot breath. The latest victim has been my typewriter, and minus it I am like a steamship without its propeller.

It was a sirocco day, and I was typing

rather vigorously, when my old friend suddenly gave out. For sixteen years it has been my faithful and obedient servant, and travelled far on my knee, and clicked to the music of American trains. Neither the heights of the Rockies nor the hustle of Seattle ever affected its serenity; but there, of course, there is no sirocco.

I was in the middle of a sentence when it failed me. I enquired diligently for a mender of Hammond typewriters. At last I discovered a man whose highest credentials were that he repaired gramophones. Is it not a characteristic of the age that the latter is more in evidence than the former? After a patient investigation he pronounced that the mainspring was broken, and depressed me by stating that another could not be got in Malta. Why do I narrate this? Because there is a study of Maltese character in it; and, as you will see, the impression this workman left was in the end not unfavourable. He took my machine to hospital, and, of course, during that time my brain was very fertile with

Malta Rainbows

ideas, the article I could have written you then would really have interested, the thoughts were on the very tips of my fingers, but, alas! there were no keyboards at hand, and so all those bright imaginations were lost.

At last the typewriter returned, but only in a convalescent state. The mechanic could get it to work—but only if one end was elevated at an angle of forty-five degrees. He was triumphant. I was not so enthusiastic. But as I wished to catch up on those fleeting ideas, and could wait no longer, I propped one side of my convalescent machine up with books and started.

Like most people I have had my share of provocations in life—I play golf a little —but never has my temper been tested so sorely. Cruel are the wounds of a friend. I had just got hold of the tail end of an idea, and was imprisoning it in a sentence, when the carriage of the Hammond stopped, and I had to give it a push with my thumb. This diverted my thoughts, and by that time the idea had escaped to fairyland. This happened frequently, and always at a critical moment. My ideas just teased me, they laughed at me from a safe distance, and with a convalescent typewriter I was powerless to catch them. So I sent it back to hospital again, and the Maltese mechanic who had already shown one characteristic of his race, now revealed the counter-balancing virtue of deft and painstaking manipulation. He took the machine to pieces. He joined the parts of the broken mainspring; how I do not know, and he has returned it to me in as perfect working condition as the day sixteen years ago when it first stepped brand new from the counter into my desk.

And now for my subject. Three large Army books lie before me filled with the names of patients to whom it has been my privilege to minister. Some of them are home again, others are back at the front; many have gone where there is no more sorrow or sighing. They are all more than names. They have become memories, and as the light of memory plays upon them I see there a rainbow radiant with its Christian virtues, and I would like you to catch a glimpse of it also as it spans with its message of hope the dark cloud of suffering.

PATIENCE

How many names rank themselves under this heading! I could play on your heartstrings by telling you of scores who preached its silent sermon; and if I should ever get impatient again I have only to think of them and feel ashamed.

One face I recall that used to light up with its smile of welcome. It was that of a man whose legs, whose arms, whose neck, were paralysed, so that the only part of him he could move was his eyes. It is his smile that haunts me to-night. On such a background it almost seemed out of place, but that was the fascination of it. He never complained. He liked you to come and talk with him. To sit down at his bedside as if you really meant a chat. He answered with those wonderful eyes of his. I have seen humour play in their depths, but never did I notice the darkening of impatience. One day I went to his ward as usual, and found him away. He was gone, and yet not gone. He had been marked down for England for some time.

"Left yesterday in a hospital ship," was what his neighbour told me. Yet somehow he still seemed to be in the ward. He had left behind him the subtle charm of his wonderful patience. That was months ago, and now a new generation are in these beds who know not "Joseph." Still I fancy he is there, for something about the ward distinguishes it from others. There is the aroma of a gracious sufferer. I cannot explain it, but somehow all its patients seem more gentle, more submissive.

Those who knew him spoke often about his patience. One by one they left, but the tradition remained of the man in bed No. 3. It would be a happy thing to think that here we had a parable of life, and that one day, when the place that knows us shall know us no more, there will be left behind something that will cling to that spot, something that will unconsciously influence others, something more than a memory—an aroma, if you like to call it so.

COURAGE

Here again I can have my pick of pages. What stories of battles I have heard at first hand! Let me take you to the bedside of a sergeant of the Ayrshire Yeomanry, and listen to an account of one of the pluckiest deeds ever wrought, which is not without its touch of humour.

It was during what must have been one of our very last attacks at Cape Helles. Some of the enemy's saps were being taken. In one of them the Turks turned to the left and rushed for a barricade their friends had reared. The British gave chase, but it was necessary to investigate the turning to the right, down which a few Turks were seen to run, in case it connected with a Turkish trench. It really did, but a shell at that moment burst and blew it in, blocking the passage. The sergeant started to explore. A few minutes later a shell knocked in the sap behind him, so that he could not re-

Malta Rainbows

turn. On rounding a barricade of sandbags what was his amazement to find about thirty Turks grouped in the sap, which had been made a cul-de-sac by the bursting shell. He had not a moment in which to make up his mind. He knew that he could not go back, and to go forward meant thirty to one. However, he kept his presence of mind, and lowering his rifle to impress them with the fact that he felt too confident of his superiority even to threaten them, he called upon them to surrender. They imagined that he was the leader of a large party of British troops, and, realising that they were in a tight corner, they dropped their weapons and raised their hands. Thus he held them while the battle raged at the other end of the sap and until a way was cleared behind him. Then he motioned to them to come forward one by one, and as each Turk passed him his enemy patted him on the back in gratitude for having spared their lives!

A tale like that tells of nerve, and it was very simply narrated to me by the sergeant, who, I am sure, would blush to see it repeated in print.

CHEERFULNESS

I might choose at random any of the several thousand names before me, and use it as an illustration of this virtue. What is the secret of this almost unquenchable cheerfulness in our British soldier? I have seen it asserted under very strange circumstances. The other day one poor fellow came into our club. He had both his hands shot away, and was unable to feed himself. Yet he sat down at a table, and seemed greatly to relish the cup of tea held to his lips by a comrade's hands. He talked and laughed with the others, and appeared thoroughly to enjoy himself, and to one of the ladies whose tone questioned more than her words he replied: "What is the use of being down-hearted?" This spirit, I believe, if its origin be sought for, will be found to have its roots in the Christian faith of our country, whose fruits are sacrifice and hope.

Malta Rainbows

But one soldier stands out from the others as the cheeriest man I ever met. He was a big, handsome New Zealander, named Fraser, and when he first came in he was in a most critical condition. He had eighteen wounds in his body.

"Oh, I am getting on all right," was his first greeting to me.

From the start I noticed that his mind always dwelt on the most favourable symptoms of his wounds, and I believe that this helped to save his life.

If his shoulder were healing he spoke about that, and said nothing about his knee, which was suppurating. I called him the cheeriest patient in Valletta Hospital. When I told him about our tearoom for the wounded he insisted on giving some money to drive up some of the other men in the ward who were strong enough to go though unable to walk, and from that time onward, while battling with pain, he was always anxious to talk about it, and plan for others enjoying its benefits. For months he lay there, emitting, like radium,

CONVALESCENT CAMP, GHAIN TUFFIEHA.

Malta Rainbows

rays of cheer that brightened the whole ward. He was taken from his bed to the New Zealand hospital ship, and our last glimpse of him was a smile. That was one of Malta's rainbows, which I shall never forget.

I have seen its light in strange places. One was in the eyes of a grizzled Irishman in St. Elmo Hospital.

"How are you getting on?" I asked.

"Och! It's my eye that's bothering me. I got a chill in it last night," he answered. And yet just two days before he had had his leg amputated!

FAITH

It is with hesitating hand that I venture to draw for you a sketch of a face that looks out of my mental album at the very mention of faith. He was on the dangerous list when I first saw him, and had just arrived. There was a terrible wound in his head; yet he could speak. At first my heart grew sad as I listened to his story.

Malta Rainbows

He had neither father nor mother, nor apparently any relative. His only friend was his landlady in Scotland. He gave me her name, and told me how good she had been to him, and how sorry he felt that the war had cost her her lodger. Poor lad!

Then a word of mine brought a gleam of brightness into those eyes shadowed for the moment by the thought of his only friend. I had spoken of the Future. Already he was in the Valley of the Shadow, and in a few hours was to pass out at its other end. But if ever there was a reflector of heavenly light, a proof of the Eternal Day beyond the shades, it was that bandaged face which was catching the beauty of the sunrise. A moment before I had thought him lonely, but unconsciously he let me see the shadows of an innumerable company of angels. It is not merely at Mons that these may be observed. In the hospitals of Malta a strange brightness passes like a sunbeam across a dying face. Is it not the shadow of an angel, or of One whom the angels worship?

Malta Rainbows

ENDURANCE

One bed I must take you to, where it seems to me all the virtues I have already spoken of have a noble illustration with this one added, namely, endurance. It is six months now since Hamilton was admitted to St. Elmo Hospital. In that time he has endured seventeen operations. If you wish to know the price of war you learn it here. If you want to witness its triumph, here is one. At present he has a steel bar through his knee. But that is nothing to what there has been. Only the determination, such as our nation is now manifesting, to endure to the end could have pulled him through. Approach that bed as you would do a throne, for there the spirit of our race is being crowned, albeit with a circlet of thorns for the moment, yet with a regal dignity that denotes the conqueror.

It is the chaplain who gets at first hand those tales which, like the garments of the wounded man, are smirched with the stains of blood and still smell of powder. The doctors and nurses are occupied with the care of the poor, shattered limbs, but it is the chaplain who comes with healing for mind and soul, and if he has the sympathetic art he will realise that part of that healing process consists in listening.

The poor fellow who has just been carried from the stretcher into the bed, and who feels the comforting touch of clean sheets after he has wakened up from his first sleep, wants to tell somebody all that has happened. The exciting scenes through which he has passed have dazzled his mind, and just as one who has looked on the sun can see nothing else for a while, so the after impression of those awful sights cannot be removed until expressed in speech. After the story has once been told the mind is relieved, and it may be that the soldier will not care to speak of the subject again, for the memory is too painful.

Thus the chaplain from the bedside sees the battle at many points. He sees what one soldier saw, and then what another witnessed, and the minor incidents which

Malta Rainbows

make the battle, and which are known only to the individual, who was the principal actor in them, unfold themselves and reproduce the lurid panorama.

Let me give you some such incidents and in this grim struggle, where physical and spiritual realities become one, we will see the latter illustrated in the former.

THE POWER OF PRAYER AND COMRADESHIP

He told me the story simply as he lay wounded in nine places. It happened in an attack on the Turkish trenches. Just as the last one was being rushed three rifle bullets pierced his shoulder. He swayed and fell in front of his men, and at that moment a bomb exploded, the shrapnel hitting him in six other places and knocking him over into the communication trench. Then he swooned, and knew nothing of what was happening. Owing to a retirement at another part of the line the British force had to give up some of the trenches so dearly won, and the major was left for dead amongst a heap of the slain. When he awoke it was hours afterwards. Day had long since broken, and there was a deathly stillness round him. He was entangled in a mass of dead men, and could not move. As he turned his head he suddenly saw two Turks peering cautiously round the end of the trench at him. As soon as their eyes met the Turks "made a bunk," to use his own phrase, and then he swooned again. Once more he regained consciousness, and there were the same two Turks, a little nearer this time. He had no weapon within reach, even if he had possessed strength enough to use it; but again he looked them straight in the face, and the men fled out of sight, though every now and then they would put their heads round the corner. Evidently they had a wholesome fear, even of a wounded Briton. Then matters became more serious. The Turks threw a hand bomb over the trench at him. It struck a dead soldier and exploded without hurting the major; but he realised that to remain a moment longer where he was meant death. But how could he move?

Malta Rainbows

One thing only could he do, and that was to pray. He asked God for strength, and it was strangely given to him. He managed to get on his hands and feet and crawl a few yards, just in the nick of time, for the next bomb fell where he had been. Slowly and painfully he dragged himself along the continuation trench. Then he came on one of his own men lying helplessly wounded.

"I am afraid I have no strength left to help you," said the major sympathetically, " but if I reach anywhere this way I'll send out assistance." The man had given himself up for dead, but the voice of his officer rallied his spirit, and when the major looked round again he saw the private crawling after him. Then they met a sand-bag barrier. They were too weak to climb over it, but together they got hold of one of the bags and toppled it down, and after a rest they did the same with another. Meanwhile the Turks were cautiously stalking their prey. There was not a moment to lose. Praying for further strength, the major and private helped each other through the gap they had made in the barrier, and rolled down into another trench. Fortunately they had fallen among friends. Some men of the Essex Regiment happened to be on the other side, and they were carried to safety.

Such was the thrilling tale the wounded officer told me, and need I add that it is one more example of the power of prayer?

Ask, and ye shall receive." Also, does it not illustrate the encouragement of comradeship? The private had lost hope as well as strength, and was gasping his life out, until the words and example of his major revived his spirit, and he made the effort that saved his life. Christ does not say merely "Take up thy cross." Had He done so our hearts might have failed, but He adds, "Follow Me." He has gone before, and in that there is the stimulus that comes from comradeship.

A REFLECTION OF THE CROSS

Another lad had a strange story to tell, and the wounded men beside him were able

Malta Rainbows

to corroborate his statement. A fierce battle was raging, and in face of overwhelming numbers the British force was retiring to their trenches. Suddenly the lad heard the cry of a wounded man calling for water. He stopped and stooped over the prostrate form. Meanwhile bullets were whizzing on every side. Quickly he unslung his water bottle and held it to the other's parched lips.

"Only drink half," he said; "I may yet need the other half myself."

Then, taking pity on the wounded man, and knowing that it would likely mean death to be left out there exposed to the enemy's fire, he called a comrade and asked him to give him a hand in trying to carry the helpless soldier to shelter. Together they staggered under their load, the target now of many bullets. At last they reached the trench, and simply rolled their living burden over, then hastened to spring after him. At that instant a shell caught the rescuer on the shoulder, shattering the bone, and he fell beside the man he had helped.

His prophecy was true; he needed the other half of the bottle.

Days passed, during which the narrator of the story was carried down to the beach, put on board ship, and brought to Malta. He was taken to Cottonera Hospital, and it was there that I found him, and that the strange sequel of the story took place.

One day a wounded soldier, who is now convalescent, entered the ward. Suddenly he stopped in surprise at the first bed on his left, and looked curiously at the pale face on the pillow.

"Why, you are my rescuer!" he exclaimed with delight; "the man who gave me that drink, which I will never forget, and which I can never repay."

They did not know each other's names, but that mattered little, blood had cemented a friendship stronger than death. The half-bottle of water and the heroic deed are already reaping their reward in life's richest gift of a loyal comradeship. Thus the Cross is casting its reflection on our blood-stained fields.

Malta Rainbows

THE PRECIOUSNESS OF A PEBBLE

Our ideas of values are getting strangely upset by this war. What we are apt to consider worthless things suddenly assume an importance which teaches us that nothing which can truly serve mankind is common or unclean in the Creator's eyes. What is there more paltry than a pebble? We spurn it with our feet. Yet the story a soldier told me shows how a pebble may be above rubies to a wounded man.

In a charge in which valour had overleapt discretion a certain regiment had suddenly to halt and fall back. In an out-of-the-way hollow it left behind two wounded men. Both were injured in arms and legs, and with difficulty crawled toward each other for the comfort of companionship. When day broke and they raised their heads to look round, what was their dismay to find that they were lying within the Turkish lines. At any moment they might be discovered. Their only chance was to keep in the shelter of the hollow and

Malta Rainbows

lie flat, without moving more than possible. They shared what remaining water they had, and then nerved themselves to face the burning thirst of the blistering day. One had picked up a smooth pebble, and this he put into his mouth and sucked, and it helped to cool his tongue. Then he handed it to his comrade, and, turn about, through all that terrible day the precious pebble was exchanged from the one to the other. It was all the refreshment they had. For another night of agony and day of despair that pebble was their one solace. At last another British charge brought them within reach of friends and they were rescued along with that precious pebble, which will be cherished with greater regard than even if it were a gem. The neglected stone has been given chief place.

HOME, SWEET HOME

I close, not with a trench story, but with one that saddened and touched me deeply. Yesterday, as usual, I was summoned to many death-beds, all fever cases. I stood

Malta Rainbows

beside one man who could scarcely speak. Already his flesh had turned black, and the flies were claiming their victim. As I spoke to him he made a feeble motion with his hand towards his one treasure. It was tied up in his pocket handkerchief. I understood, and untied the knot, and took out the contents. They consisted of a crushed picture postcard and his Testament. It was the card he wished to look at again. It was an ordinary print, depicting a mother and children seated beside the hearth, and above them in a cloud the visionary scene of their thoughts, a body of soldiers marching to war. Below was printed the inscription, "It is not like home when Daddy is away."

The soldier nodded when I asked if he were a married man. He had a wife and four children. Their wait for him will, I fear, be a long one, unless the fervent prayer for the sick brings an answer which, to human minds, would seem miraculous. Such are the sacrifices that are being made —wife, children, home, life—for the sake of Empire and God.

CHAPTER VI

IN LIGHTER VEIN

TO all boys and girls who believe in the power of fairies to grant "a wish that is wished" I would utter a solemn warning. In the foolish days of my first arrival in Malta I wished a wish, and some malevolent fairy has seen to it that it has been answered. Like the mosquitoes, the post seeks to make newcomers its victims. It has a trick of tormenting the homesick stranger by allowing him no letters for what seems like weeks. Thus it extorted from me a wish. I wrote to a friend saying that I wanted letters, and I think at that the fairy must have laughed, for it hurried away with its wish, and for the last three weeks it has never ceased with evil delight to grant that foolish

In Lighter Vein

request. Even in my dreams, if I have partaken of a Maltese supper, I am haunted by my orderly's voice saying, "The Post Office officials have sent to say that they have twenty sacks waiting for you!"

That fairy is not like the mean man described by a Highlander who, in referring to his method of treating, said, "He is this sort, when you say, Stop! he stops." My post bags are weekly increasing in number, and show no signs of decrease. The D.A.A.G. asked me if I meant to run a G.P.O. as a show of my own. Yet what a pathetic sidelight on the war these heaped-up postbags are! How expressive of the patriotism, the personal anxieties of thousands in Australia and New Zealand! Malta, where their sons are lying fighting with death, is a sacred spot to them. Their hearts are here with their loved ones. Hence the mail bags.

A CHAPLAIN'S MAIL

Humour is not entirely absent even from these August days, and perhaps when I tell

In Lighter Vein

you about my weekly mail you will smile, as did Major Lyle, of the Argyll and Sutherland Highlanders, who happened to be at my house when it arrived.

The postman brought word that he was unable to bring all the correspondence that was awaiting me. The suspicion of a smile about his lips aroused my curiosity. I sent my orderly to the post office to get the letters, and he came back with nothing except the same smile. I thought then that it was time to go myself. I was escorted to the sorting-room and met there by smiling officials. Really that smile was growing infectious. Then I was conducted to my mail. It was contained in two huge sacks, four feet high. There were some lesser packages, but those sacks fascinated me. Two men could with difficulty lift one. In fact, it took three to carry it down to a cab. Where to empty out its contents was the next question when it had arrived at my house. No table could possibly hold it. The orderly hesitated about suggesting the floor, but there

In Lighter Vein

was no other place ; and so my study was turned into a General Post Office. It was then Major Lyle arrived, and I took him to see the first consignment, and I am glad I had him for a witness, otherwise I would have refrained from arousing suspicion as to my veracity. The Major was sitting in the drawing-room when the second sack arrived. He heard its laborious ascent of the stairs, and I took him out to the landing to see it. I am sorry that I did not measure its length. I cannot remember ever seeing a sack so long or fat before. My orderly has the spirit of neatness, and he built a stack on my study floor that would have delighted the heart of any farmer. The only disadvantage is that it must be unloaded from the top. I tried to count the contents of the bag and got to over two hundred and then stopped, considering it a waste of time.

Now what, you will be asking, is the meaning of this large mail. It was addressed to the Presbyterian Chaplain, and nine-tenths and more came from Australia and New

In Lighter Vein

Zealand. It is a visible expression of the loyalty of these Colonies, of how their hearts have followed their sons. The majority of the separate items were papers for wounded soldiers, addressed to the care of the chaplain. There were letters besides, asking for information about men whose whereabouts were unknown or who were in Malta.

Now, I do not wish any Scottish reader to be dissuaded from sending me the papers which are so much appreciated. We have need for them all and more. Nothing helps to brighten a wounded Scot so much as a paper from home, and I feel deeply grateful for those which are sent, and I can assure the senders that all are put to a most useful purpose.

Whether this Australian mail is to be like the high tides, a monthly affair, I cannot yet say. I am hurriedly getting rid of the rakings of the stack in fear of a weekly return of the sacks. There is a constant dribble in of papers, but last week certainly touched high-water mark. I have a vague suspicion as to its cause. I did send a copy

In Lighter Vein

of one of my Scotch articles to an Australian paper, perhaps that might have something to do with it. The real secret of course is sympathy with our wounded.

Incidentally it led me into an altercation with the chief of the post office. Many of the senders had put nothing in the address to indicate that the papers were for wounded men, many were sent simply to myself. The majority were stamped, yet several of these were underpaid. Here was the Post Office's chance for sending in a little bill and threatening me with bankruptcy! None of us like to pay excess postage on the receipt of our mail, and certainly not a Scot. So I objected, and correspondence led at last to a most courteous interview with the postmaster. My argument was for the spirit as opposed to the letter of the regulations. Technically he was right. I was not wounded. I replied that I was the representative of the wounded. He argued the needs of the post office earning an honest penny. The receipts had gone down and the expenses doubled owing to these new regulations. I had as good an argument on those lines. One had only to compare the excess postage with the pay of a chaplain to realise that the post office had not struck a very lucrative mine! It was a most pleasant interview, and had a pleasant ending—for me. The red tape had snapped, and the letter had yielded to the spirit. There was a compromise but only of detail. I was to show my respect for red tape by signing on each delivery, " for the wounded."

At this very moment, strange to say, an interruption has occurred. It is a coincidence that adds point to what I have just said. I have stopped clicking my typewriter, and the maid has given her message.

" The postmaster has sent me to say that there are two sacks of correspondence waiting at the office for you, sir."

So now I know that my mail is to be weekly, and that unless I am particularly active I shall soon have a perfect farmyard of paper stacks in my study.

Months have passed since I wrote the

In Lighter Vein

above, and so I am now able to add the sequel. What I have described has been but the neap tide. Every week has not failed to bring its twenty sacks. Once we had thirty-five, but that was high-water mark.

How are they disposed of? is, I have no doubt, the question in your mind. Some I take home, and hand over to the stack-building talents of my orderly; others I had transferred to our Soldiers' Club. There were about sixty men in at the time, some reading, others writing, some playing games.

Surmising what would happen, I got the bags quietly placed at intervals in the lobby. Then entering I announced that an Australian and New Zealand mail had just come in, and that I had several bags with papers outside, and that those present could help themselves, and take what they liked back to their hospitals. You should have witnessed the scene that followed. Books, tables, ink and writing pads were left in a moment. I have seen flies settling on

In Lighter Vein

syrup, but that is a feeble illustration; I have seen a football scrimmage, which is nearer the mark. Round each bag there was a mass of bodies, inside were the heads and hands. These Australians appeared to know by the feel their own local paper, and one or another would emerge holding aloft in triumph what corresponds to his *Greenock Telegraph.* The best illustration of all is that of vultures descending on a carcase. In ten minutes the bags were picked bare, and lay in little collapsed heaps. A few papers were scattered round them. Scotch ones, which were discarded by the Australians, but which were very carefully collected by me and sorted out for our Scotch lads.

As for the letters, I do not care to speak of them. I am afraid that fairy is sitting on a pile of unanswered ones and laughing at me. I have heard of sea captains experiencing a strange sensation when they felt themselves mastered by the sea. My typewriter and I have been inseparable companions for years, we have crossed the

In Lighter Vein

Rockies together and wandered into many strange places, but now we feel like the sea captain, mastered by our own element. Though the keys were to work at their hardest I am afraid that pile of unanswered letters would never grow less; for no sooner with a sigh of relief do I begin to see the top of my table appearing through the heaps of envelopes, than it is hopelessly covered again; while I have been out another post has come in. However, every one has their own difficulties in these days, and if my Achi Baba is visibly entrenching itself on my desk I have yet the will to win, and some day I shall master it.

INTERESTING VISITORS

I have a feeling that my last chapters were sad, that I lifted the veil too freely which hides the grim side of war; so when I began this one I promised myself a holiday. I determined to shut the door on the day's work and speak only of its pleasures.

One of the greatest of these was the visit

In Lighter Vein

we had from our M.P., Major Godfrey Collins. We were out when he first called, but he found his way to the Soldiers' Club, and spent half an hour with Mrs. Mackinnon. Next morning he called for me, and we had a delightful chat. He is on his way East, and has utilised his few days in Malta in visiting the wounded Greenock lads. With one he had an amusing conversation.

"I remember you," he said to him, "and have good reason to. The last time we met was at a political meeting, and you heckled me."

The soldier laughed. How far away those days seem now.

"Well, I hope," added the Major, "that we may meet again as we did before, heckling and all."

"I'll let you off easier the next time, sir," was the rejoinder from the bed.

Two nights ago I had the most interesting conversation of my life. It was with a naval officer who had been spending the last forty days in the Sea of Marmora, sometimes resting on its bed. He is on a sub-

In Lighter Vein

marine. But I must not tell you all he so frankly spoke of. What his submarine alone has done is beyond words. The wonderful things his captain discovered, and how they cheated the wily Turk who tried to net them will make one of the most exciting chapters in the history of this war.

Lying at the bottom of the Sea of Marmora, shelling Turkish regiments from the sea and then diving before their guns could answer, sinking the enemy's troopships with thousands of men—how many I had better not say—breaking through the nets set to trap them—all these adventures seemed hardly to have taken the edge off the boyishness of the young naval officer. Perhaps it was because he was still so youthful that these daring deeds had for him that exhilarating thrill missed by those of thinner blood.

THE WEATHER

Now how about the climate? Is it kindly towards our wounded? The late Prof. Henry Drummond stayed once for

In Lighter Vein

a fortnight with Dr. Wisely in Malta in July, and he said tropical Africa was nothing to Malta. I am ready to agree, though I have not seen the other place. How are you getting through the heat of August then, you ask? I can only say that it is the heat that does the getting through. It never ceases to come out of one's pores and every one of them. I have discovered only one remedy for it, and that is to be too busy to even think of it. It is fatal if you let your eye rest longingly on the sofa, and sink there to meditate on the heat. You are its victim at once. Of course one often gets a rude reminder in the middle of one's forgetfulness. Especially when I feel a strange thing round my neck and put up my hand to find a circlet of pulp where only a short time before there had been a stiff starched collar, fresh from the laundry. It was rather disconcerting last Sunday to make the discovery at my fourth service when I entered the vestry at the church in Valletta. I had left only half an hour to get across

In Lighter Vein

from my service at Bighi, and the only dghaisa I could get was manned by one old man. I would have taken an oar only the thought of my collar restrained me. I might have done so without much difference in results, for the quarter-of-a-mile hurried walk effectively did for it, and when I felt for a collar on which to tie my bands there was none left worthy of the name. There is only one place where one escapes from the heat, and even then I have my doubts. The first thing you make for on getting home is a cold bath. By that time you are in an extravagant mood and forget that every drop of water is charged for, and, with a wild joy, fill the bath, but even when you get completely under the cold water I am not quite sure whether you are not still perspiring!

THE MOSQUITOES

The mosquitoes, harbingers of summer, have returned in force. Like the rising generation, one doubts whether they are better than their grandparents of last

In Lighter Vein

summer. In fact, they are just chips of the old block, as Americans would say, and are busy with their old game. My respect, however, for them has increased. I do not know whether Malta mosquitoes are wiser than their cousins of other regions. I have been compelled to undertake a painful study of them, and alas! it is no second-hand evidence I offer you. Personal investigations have been forced upon me, and reluctantly I have discovered that the Malta mosquito has a wonderful brain.

This is how he goes about his business. As you are at a safe distance it will not unduly pain you if I narrate something of his frightfulness. He alights on my cheek when I am half awake, and lowers his long proboscis, which resembles somewhat an elephant's trunk, and extends its divided lobes until they get a firm grip of the skin. Then he is ready for action, and is as happy as a surgeon who has a delicate operation in hand. Inside this proboscis are five knives, with which he begins to cut a way through the flesh, going deeper and deeper until the

In Lighter Vein

blood spurts out. Now he inserts a tube, through which he sucks up the blood. If this were all the damage he did we might be content with calling him a mere marauder, and not a murderer. But, unfortunately, he is playing the German game here, and many of our casualties are due to him. You see he does not take the care he ought when he goes from person to person, and, unlike a good surgeon, leaves his lancets unwiped. The consequence is that he carries germs from the blood of one man to another. These may be virulent microbes, that benefit by the change, and in their new surroundings reproduce themselves in millions, and thus cause fever. The particular braininess of the Maltese mosquito is in the crafty way he smuggles himself in the daytime through the net, and hides under your pillow until the propitious moment, when you are sound asleep. Only in his case there is this compensation, he does not know when to stop, and gorges himself to such an extent that his sin finds him out. In the morning he

In Lighter Vein

is weighted with his repast. Revenge has its chance, and that is an end of him.

HUMOROUS STORIES

The Hospital Ward is perhaps the last place where you would expect to come across funny incidents. Possibly the sombre background heightens by contrast what humour there is, and gives it greater piquancy.

One very opinionative patient was cruelly rebuked by a slip of the orderly's pen. I asked him what religion he was, and for answer he looked at me very superiorly and said, "I am a Rationalist."

"Oh, I understand," I replied. "I could not just quite make out what was written on your card."

We took it down for closer inspection, and found that the orderly in his haste or his army love for contraction had written, "Religion—RAT."

Another on being asked what he was suffering from quite innocently answered, "C.O.E."

Again the orderly had been in a hurry

In Lighter Vein

and had inserted his religious denomination in the space left for the description of his disease, and the patient I suppose had been wondering what kind of strange illness these letters indicated.

This story reminds me of another. A patient when asked by Rev. W. Cowan what his disease was, answered, " Well, I don't quite know. I have had three specialists looking at me and they don't seem to know either. You can put me down as a medical curio."

This leads up to the story told by Mr. W. M. Grant, one of our Guild workers. A man said to him in the tent one day, " I've had seeven dochtors, an' been rubbit wi' seeven different kinds o' lotions, an' forbye a' that I have had three peels, an' I'm no a whit the better."

Rev. C. McEchern was passing through one of the tents in St. Patrick's Camp on St. Patrick's day, and came on a typical Irish soldier looking very disconsolate.

" You ought to be in better spirits on St. Patrick's day," he said.

In Lighter Vein

"I am not of his persuasion," was the glum response.

The difficulties of the chaplain have sometimes their sadly humorous aspect. Mr. Cowan was visiting a Welshman the other day who was very ill.

"Have you written to your wife?" he asked.

"No, I am not able. Will you do it?"

"Yes, but you must give me her address."

For answer there came curious guttural sounds from the man's throat. The chaplain bent his head as near as possible but could make nothing of them.

"Spell it," he said at last in desperation, for the man's strength was sinking, and this is the entry that stands in the chaplain's notebook:

"C C L L H W R Y Y——"

The Scot is not supposed to be very quick at repartee, but loyalty will sharpen any man's wits, as it did the lad to whom Mr. Cowan handed a magazine with the picture of an actress on its cover.

"There is a pretty girl to look at," he said.

ENTRANCE TO PIETA CEMETERY

In Lighter Vein

"Aye, but I ken whar thar's a bonnier ane," was the retort of the true-hearted lad, who was thinking of the girl he had left behind him.

He was more chivalrous than his fellow-countryman, to whom the same chaplain put the question, "Are you married?"

"Na, na!" was the ungallant answer. "Fechtin' the Turks is quite enough by itsel'."

There was grim point to the reply given by a wounded soldier, who had been enduring intense agony, when asked how he felt. "Just as I wad lik' twa men to feel —the Kaiser an' the Crown Prince."

From the mail-bag one might pick out many tit-bits of unconscious humour. Here is an extract from a letter by a lady written to one of our chaplains. "My son is in a Malta hospital suffering from dysentery. The last time he had it the doctor ordered him half a pound of best rump steak daily. Will you see that he gets it?"

Another commission for the chaplain was as follows, "Do you think you could

In Lighter Vein

possibly trace a pair of pyjamas, which I sent to my son who was in a hospital in Malta?"

So the shadows have their glimpses of sunshine, and a laugh is occasionally heard where it sounds strangely.

THE BELLS

But there go the bells : For months they have been silent, and visitors did not know they were in Valletta. Harder than for many a busy gossip has it been for them to keep their tongues tied, and now St. John's has broken loose. Of course it is September 8, and all who read their histories know that Valletta could not keep silent on that historic date.

> " Oh the bells, bells, bells,
> What a tale their terror tells
>   Of despair!
> How they clang, and clash, and roar,
> What a horror they outpour
>   On the bosom of the palpitating air!"

If on September 8, 1565, they rang as they are doing now I do not wonder that the Turks ran away. From May 18 to

In Lighter Vein

September 8 the ships and armies of Solyman the Magnificent besieged this island fortress. Opposed to him was a small band of the Knights of St. John, headed by their Grand Master, the great La Valette. Never has personal character or skilful leadership inspired men more. La Valette was everywhere. Although the world realised it not he was fighting almost single-handed the critical action of that great contest with the followers of Mohammed, whose rearguard action is being fought to-day. La Valette first broke the power of Turkey on the rocky cliffs of Malta.

> "Vain are the efforts of fierce Othman's hordes,
> They bite the dust ; they see above them fly
> The banner of the Cross upheld by swords
> Of men resolved to conquer or to die."

On the morning of that September 8 the bells broke into a laugh and the people wept for joy. Not a warrior but was wounded, not a wall but was reddened with blood ; but the Turks had turned and fled. They did not know how near victory they were ;

In Lighter Vein

how little blood there was still left to be shed. The valour of La Valette and his knights had awed them, and their commander feared less the wrath of the disappointed Solyman than the swords of those men who set the world an example of how to die. The inspiration of that thrilling victory is left not merely to the bells to repeat; an Italian poet has caught its spirit in his address to the Maltese youth :—

" Let evermore that stainless glory shine
    Before your eyes—the glory of your sires;
And in your hearts, as in a sacred shrine,
    Burn evermore their patriot warrior fires!

Oh, may the story of that deathless fight
    Still make you like your fathers, brave and strong;
May some great minstrel shape the tale aright
    And tell it to the world in deathless song."

CHAPTER VII

ORGANISATION

MEDICAL

THE development of the hospital accommodation of Malta has been one of the remarkable achievements of the great war. At the beginning of May 1915 only a few hundred beds were available for the use of the sick and wounded soldiers. In the succeeding months those resident or on duty in Malta were witnesses of a wonderful pageant—the opening of hospital after hospital till at the end of November 1915 the island could accommodate 20,000 patients, and actually did house that number. With a little more effort the number of beds could easily have been increased to 25,000, and the plans and material for this increase

Organisation

were ready. In all twenty-seven hospitals and camps were established, including Ghain Tuffieha, which in itself contained four camps holding 4,000 men.

This development of hospitals, all admirably staffed with medical officers and nurses and equipped with everything that was necessary for the welfare of the sick and wounded, was due to the energy and administrative skill of Colonels Sleman and Cumming. They worked under the fostering guidance of His Excellency, Lord Methuen, whose extraordinary activity, enthusiasm, sympathy and wisdom in counsel are known to all workers in Malta. Surgeon-General Whitehead arrived in August, and energetically furthered the work on. Malta was fortunate in the officers who came to serve her, but behind all the brains and organisation so complete was the heart of the Governor, which imparted the inspiration and driving force which made all the machinery run sweetly.

Engraved on His Excellency's heart must be the motto, "Labor ipse voluptas,"

Organisation

for he has won all hearts by his untiring and incessant labours, visiting with the regularity of a chaplain one hospital every day, and cheering the wounded with ready words of encouragement, and many a happy sally. The motto I have quoted gives the key of the reason why all in Malta love him, and are proud to serve under him.

It is impossible adequately to describe the wonderful work that has been done in Malta. The reader should remember that everything had to be imported into the island, which, after all, is but a bare rock, not supplying in peace time sufficient food for the inhabitants, and growing only vegetables, grain, fruit, poultry and goats! Nevertheless the sick and wounded soldier never lacked any comfort or luxury which would aid his recovery.

In the summer of 1915 the hospitals were staffed by nearly 300 medical officers, and the nursing sisters reached almost 1,000 in number. Over the latter was Miss Hoadley. She was assisted by the matrons of the different hospitals. In the strenuous

Organisation

days they were almost swept off their feet with the sudden inrush of nurses. To appoint these to their several stations, and select for promotion those especially qualified for larger responsibilities, required quick judgment of character as well as business-like gifts. Everywhere and at all times the medical officers and nursing sisters seemed to illustrate in their daily life the concluding words of a remarkable passage in Stevenson's "El Dorado"—" And the true success is to labour."

About one-half of the nursing sisters were V.A.D.'s, or only partly trained nurses; but without their self-sacrificing labours the sick and wounded could not have been properly looked after and nursed. It is only right to say that these so-called partly trained ladies did superb work on many critical occasions, and that many of them were highly educated, and had made big sacrifices in relinquishing home and comforts at the call of duty to nurse the British soldier.

The fully qualified nurses had a great

Organisation

strain put upon them when the sudden inrush of wounded came, but they rose to the occasion manfully. The adjective fits the case, for to all the feminine qualities of tenderness and sympathy which are necessary for a nurse there must be added something almost masculine, not merely strength of muscle, but a firmness of will, and powers of quick decision. These were manifested in the hospitals of Malta. The matrons especially, exercised a strong influence in their several spheres. In charge of Valletta Hospital, and also of the largest home for nurses was Miss Brown, and she discharged the duties of her dual office with thoroughness and industry. Miss McFarlane who left St. Patrick's Camp, for St. Andrew's Hospital, and then for the Front, was the subject of many letters of gratitude in the local press from her patients, and the sorrow at her departure was one of the finest testimonies to the power and influence of a good and clever woman in a position of authority. In another chapter I refer to Miss McDougall, who has since

Organisation

been promoted from Ghain Tuffieha Camp to Cottonera Hospital. The blend of gentleness and firmness, the happy knack of putting patients and nurses at their ease in her presence, is not only characteristic of her, but of the other matrons in Malta, whose success has depended so much on mixing in right proportions the official and human elements in their nature.

In the high pressure of work night and day last summer Ruskin's words may be used as descriptive of the Medical Officers and Nursing Sisters of the Malta Command of the British Army :—" Adventuring for man's sake apart from all reward they seem to long at once to save mankind, to make some unexampled sacrifice on their behalf, to bring some wondrous good from heaven or earth for them or perish winning eternal weal in the act," and indeed death took toll both of Medical Officers and Nursing Sisters.

To one of these I must allude for I have experienced a personal loss in the death of Lieutenant McGowan, of Grangemouth,

Organisation

who was stationed at St. George's Hospital. From the start he offered to help me in all my work, and during the months when I was single-handed he and Captain MacKinnon took practically the work of St. George's off my shoulders. Busy enough with their medical duties, they yet never missed a service they could possibly attend, setting a splendid example to their patients, which was followed. Lieutenant McGowan was seized with fever, and his illness was short. It was my sad privilege to wait on him during those days, and witness as heroic a death as any on the battlefield. The same night I officiated at his funeral, which was one of the largest I have yet seen on the island, as he was laid to rest in peaceful Pieta with all military honours.

A word must be added in praise of the British Army Medical Administration under Sir Alfred Keogh, K.C.B. When the first consulting surgeon arrived in May 1915 on the island he came with this message from the Director-General, " We wish to bring to the humblest soldier the best

Organisation

available surgery, and that which is not the best is not good enough."

During 1915 the following Senior Consultants worked on the island.

Colonel Charles Ballance, Surgeon to St. Thomas' Hospital.

Colonel Charters Symonds, Surgeon to Guy's Hospital.

Colonel Thorburn, Surgeon to the Manchester Royal Infirmary.

Colonel Purves Stewart, Physician to Westminster Hospital.

Colonel Gulland, Physician to the Edinburgh Royal Infirmary.

Colonel Garrod, Physician to St. Bartholomew's Hospital.

These men worked as a band of brothers. All serious cases were by order at once notified to them by telephone and were visited, and consultations held. No serious operation or amputation was allowed to be performed without consultation. Every hospital was visited at least twice a week by the physicians and surgeons; and methodical visits to the wards and to all

Organisation

cases were made as is the custom in peace time in all the great hospitals. Sunday was no exception, and on that day rest was no more possible in the hospitals than on week-days. The labours of the consultants were incessant, and often extended far into the night.

In the subordinary sciences, which are so essential to the investigation of disease and injury, such as pathology, bacteriology, and radiography the island was well supplied by Sir Alfred Keogh with able and earnest scientific workers. These by their labours immensely assisted in unravelling difficult and obscure problems in Clinical diagnosis and treatment; and thus in every conceivable manner the welfare and recovery of the sick and wounded soldier was provided for.

RECREATION TENTS

If you do not kill time, time will kill you. The man who has nothing to do grows prematurely old. Health-making is a complex art: it requires not merely the surgeon

Organisation

and his bottles, but stimulus for mind and spirit.

His Excellency, Lord Methuen, was quick to realise that fact, and welcomed most gratefully the offer of Recreation Tents for the wounded, when at the end of June 1915 I suggested the matter to him. The Guild of the United Free Church of Scotland responded to my request by sending out two thoroughly equipped tents, well staffed by men experienced in such work.

The great organisation of the Y.M.C.A. was not idle in the matter, and soon they had a dozen or more tents on the island with a staff of thirty workers. In a subsequent chapter I refer to the organising skill of Mr. Wilson, who so ably laid the foundations of the successful work carried on by the Y.M.C.A. A better man could not have been sent to break ground, and quickly he won the high esteem and confidence of all from His Excellency the Governor to the private who found in him a true friend, and the sorrow at his departure was universal.

Organisation

He was succeeded by Mr. Wheeler who quickly developed the work. His Excellency the Governor gave the Y.M.C.A. a suite of rooms in the Palace Buildings for Head Quarters, and with the assistance of motor-cars they soon had completed an organisation that left no camp uncared for, and that reflects great credit on Mr. Wheeler who has shown himself a master of detail.

His Excellency the Governor has, I know, put a generous estimate on the part performed by these tents in the recovery of the men. Without those centres of recreation and fellowship life under canvas would have been dreary enough, especially in the more isolated parts of the island.

In a camp where one of our Guild Tents has been placed the Commanding Officer said to me that from the day it was opened crime had diminished by 50 per cent.

ENTERTAINMENTS

But there were other things that were not overlooked. Lord Methuen has shown himself a true believer in the power of

Organisation

music to soothe and charm, and perhaps the best exponent of his theory was the Hon. Seymour Methuen, who is an accomplished violinist. She was ever ready to place her skill at the service of those who were seeking to entertain the wounded. In this connection there is one name that will be remembered by the thousands whose days of suffering were enlivened by music and song, and that is Major Hasell. He was the man behind the scenes. You had only to give him the order at short notice for a ready-made concert party, and the article was promptly supplied. What necromancer's art he possessed has been the puzzle of us all. Certainly he never failed. The Y.M.C.A. also did their best to supply this need, and their splendidly equipped concert party became very popular in all the camps.

BRITISH RED CROSS AND ORDER OF ST. JOHN

This leads me to speak of the work of one of the largest societies for the welfare of the soldiers, The British Red Cross

Organisation

and Order of St. John. Endowed with generously gifted funds and with splendid head quarters, this society pursued its work under favourable conditions. Its operations were varied. It supplied each hospital with a staff of lady visitors. These were warmly welcomed by the wounded. It also had a little gift box prepared for each arrival, containing just the things a man might need. It was the recipient of large gifts of clothing and hospital requisites for the use of the wounded, and these were distributed wherever required. It also had a concert party that did yeoman service, and in this way it carried out most successfully its aim to care for the physical and social needs of our suffering soldiers.

One great centre of entertainment was the beautiful building erected at Pembroke by money sent from the colonies, and fittingly named by His Excellency the Governor, The Australian Hall. Here the Red Cross carry on a Recreation Room for the wounded in the Pembroke district, and

Organisation

on many nights in the week the large hall is filled to overflowing with an audience of convalescents who listen with great appreciation to the entertainment of song and recitation provided for them. The Gymnasium and Soldiers' and Sailors' Home, carried on in Valletta by the Church of England, have taken their share nobly in the extra burden imposed upon them by the war, as also the Connaught Home run by the Wesleyans.

It would be impossible to speak of all the methods that have been devised for the entertainment of our wounded. Maltese ladies have been eager to help, and many a private party has been given to Tommy which the world may not hear of, but which he will not forget. The services which Mrs. Bonavia has rendered have earned the gratitude of all, and the special Tea Room at Sliema, run by her and the ladies of the Red Cross, has proved a most popular rendezvous for the convalescent soldier.

The ladies of St. Paul's Church have done their part by providing a roof tea every

Organisation

Sunday afternoon for the wounded, and this has been much appreciated by the men. While at St. Paul's Bay the wife of the colonel in command there has started a tea-room for the benefit of the troops in that neighbourhood.

Thus it will be seen that nothing has been left undone that could in any way lighten the lot of the man whose ill fortune made him fortunate enough to become one of Malta's spoiled children. But you will agree with me that they all deserved all the spoiling that could be bestowed upon them, and I am glad to say that their heads were in no way turned by it, though the postman's bag was made the heavier by the increasing number of letters of gratitude written by the men when they had rejoined their regiment, and were looking back on the good times they had had in Malta.

All this varied social work found a ready sympathiser and helper in Lady Methuen. Not only did she organise and superintend, but she visited personally the hospitals, and no visitor left a more gracious memory

Organisation

behind her. She cared for all classes. For the officers she established a homely club, where the strongest refreshment was a good cup of tea, and which was much appreciated by those who frequented it. For the soldiers she was constantly planning some new means of helping them. For the nurses, along with His Excellency, she gave up for several months their beautiful palace of St. Antonio, that the nurses might have a holiday there. These acts so thoughtful and generous can never be forgotten as long as the story of Malta's hospitals will be told.

THE ORDNANCE DEPARTMENT

Though out of sight the marvellous work of the Ordnance Department in Malta should not be out of mind. Remember two facts, that into Malta practically everything has to be imported, and that when the rush came and hospitals and camps sprang up in a night there was no time to send to England for all the necessary equipment. How was it supplied? I will take you to a

Organisation

factory that usually turns out war material only. But there were brains there as well as hands. So all turned to, and soon all kinds of hospital furniture was being produced. Here were back rests for the wounded, there full length-baths. Mosquito net poles, iron beds, motor trollies, camp tents, limber and gun carriages are but a small assortment of the medley of necessary articles that took shape in this establishment. From "a pin to a gun" or "a needle to an anchor" is how one might describe the endless variety, without which Malta would have been powerless to do its healing.

Five hundred workmen had the busiest time in their lives, and their skill and promptitude eased many a poor fellow's suffering. "We are all soldiers only wearing different uniforms," said His Excellency the Governor to them, and their willingness and devoted energy will surely not go without its reward.

CHAPTER VIII

THE VALLEY OF THE SHADOW

I CAN give it no other name. It is in the hospital wards where this Valley casts its longest and deepest shadow. On the battlefield the shadow falls, but it quickly flits past, leaving behind the hastily dug graves. Death is sudden, the Valley is robbed of its lingering terrors to some extent ; but in the hospital it is otherwise, the shadow lingers and you walk in it for days ; nay, you are never free from it. You see it gathering round this bed and that. Too well have you learned its signs, and though the brave sufferer says cheerily that " he is getting on fine," you know that already his feet are entering the Valley, and the heart yearns to light the way a little for him. To hold before him some of the Bible's gracious promises, that the dark

The Valley of the Shadow

path might be brightened, is the chaplain's greatest privilege but most trying task. To accompany the departing warrior as far as earthly footsteps can, and then to stretch out as it were the hand with the torch of Truth that the rays may guide him until, beyond the shadows, he passes into a brighter Light; it is this that causes soul strain.

The shadow I see has fallen across my manuscript—it falls everywhere here, like the dust, and if for the moment you feel its chill, my excuse must be, that if you wish to understand Malta at present you cannot escape looking into the Valley.

August has been very different from July. The funerals have now mounted up to fifteen and twenty a day. One begins the day at the graveside and ends it there. Every morning as I drive out the one mile to peaceful Pieta Cemetery I feel the revolt of Nature at this haunting of Death. At six in the morning Malta is lovely. The sun has not yet got its deadly range, and in the soft breeze one feels the wooing of life.

The Valley of the Shadow

The birds are happy, and when one hears a laugh, which is rather a rare thing here, you feel in sympathy with it. Even the solemn cypress trees that keep sad vigil over the graves seem less sombre. For the moment one feels far removed from death, all round there is an awakening to life. Then from a distance on the morning air there breaks in with its dull discord a single beat of a drum, followed solemnly by another and then another. Death is not banished, or silent, but comes to mock the beauty of life. Slowly the cortège nears, men can set their watches by it now in Malta as they hasten to their work. Not one coffin, but many are laid in the deep, stone-lined graves, and the town, as its activities begin to stir, hears again the three solemn volleys and the haunting echoes of the "Last Post," as soldiers bid farewell to their fallen comrades. The officiating chaplains part to meet again at the same place at sunset, for the same sad duties. But between these hours there is much to do.

But come with me through the wards

The Valley of the Shadow

where the Shadow falls. The recovering and the dying lie side by side. A curtain round one cot tells its own tale. Behind it the surgeon and nurses are making a final effort to rally the ebbing strength of a sinking man. But all are not in that condition. So in our survey we will leave the worst cases to the last.

From the background of Malta a great procession of faces looks out upon me. The person who stands still as the crowd goes by sees more of them than one who is actually part of the moving throng. The latter is only familiar with those around who keep step with him. A rough calculation puts the figure at about thirty thousand men with whom I have come into personal contact either through visitation or by meeting them at our Soldiers' Club. They resolve themselves into types, and perhaps a study of these might interest you.

THE OLD SOLDIER

The man who saved the Empire, who broke the back of the enemy before he got

The Valley of the Shadow

his first thrust home, all honour to the courage, and discipline, and self-sacrifice of this type of hero! We have had many here, and you can generally recognise them at a first glance.

One I have good cause for remembering. He was a sergeant in the K.O.S.B. His twenty years' service had written his certificate plainly in his face. That he had been so long in the army seemed almost impossible, so youthful he looked with his smartly trimmed moustache, though on a closer scrutiny one recognised the lines on the tanned cheeks, engraved there by strenuous efforts, acts of quick decision in many a tight corner, and by the moulding hand of discipline which gave strong character to the features.

I found it remarkably easy to win his confidence. Perhaps the fact that I happened to have in my bag his home local paper, which he had not seen for months, was a key that helped to unlock the door of his heart. He looked pretty badly wounded, and I hesitated about telling

The Valley of the Shadow

him that on Sunday morning I was going to hold a service in that hospital.

"If I can crawl along I'll come," he said.

This heartened me; and, knowing how difficult it is to start a service until it takes on amongst the men, I added "and bring any others you can."

"I'll bring 'em," was his answer.

On Sunday morning I was surprised at the size of my congregation. Never before or since have I had one like it there. The Sergeant had brought 'em. He had made his whole ward, which was a big one, turn out en masse, without any fine distinctions as to denominations of religion or oversensitive feelings for wounded limbs. Bandaged and on crutches they limped along, the Sergeant bringing up the rear leaning on two sticks. It was a tribute to the wonderful influence he had over his fellow-sufferers. He was a born leader of men, of the type generals are made if only he had had a wider education and greater opportunities.

The Valley of the Shadow

THE BOY SOLDIER

We have had them too. There are no lines on their faces, not even the buddings of a coming moustache. They have trifled with truth I fear, and followed the example of their maiden aunt, whose weak spot the census papers have discovered by manipulating their natal dates, only instead of aspiring to youth they have coveted age. The recruiting officer also, I think, has turned the blind spot in his eye on them, and so they have become men before their time. One who has been a frequenter of the club has been called " The Baby." He is proud of the title, which shows, of course, that it is inappropriate, for if there was ever a tougher little bit of humanity than this lad I have yet to discover it. There is a naïveté about his battle yarns that is delightful. His experience of the nursery has been too recent for him to see anything in the sterner realities of life than a big game. This unconsciousness was a veritable shield to his soul, which had passed

The Valley of the Shadow

through the ordeal of battle without its simplicity being marred, and yet withal he is a little piece of hard granite.

There is another who has earned the same name. He is the pet of a certain hospital. Poor boy, all the kindness and caressing are a meagre recompense for his lost limbs. His pale face, and eyes liquid in their quick tenderness of feeling, in whose depths one searches in vain for a reproach against his fate, move one strangely. He is a greater force in the world to-day than when gripping his rifle he formed but one in the long khaki line. Suffering has singled him out for distinction. He is a marked man in the ward, he will be a marked man in his whole journey through life. Voices grow more tender in his presence, rough hands vie for the honour of wheeling his chair. The men who have legs of their own and can walk up town always bring some little gift back with them for him. Four the other day said that they would lift his chair into the ferry steamer and take him for a wheel to the other side of the harbour.

The Valley of the Shadow

The nurses, I think, are jealous for his smiles. Poor, fair-haired boy, who will never walk again; he is but beginning his task. It will not be that of killing Boches. To make a gentleman of every man who meets him and a lady of every woman who enters his presence, that is to be his future rôle in life. Already he has begun well. All the men in his ward are gentlemen, and the nurses ladies, whatever they might have been before. It has been good for others to dwell under the shadow of that broken life. He is destined to be God's polisher, to refine other souls, to bring human tenderness to the surface, to make hearts the reflection of divine pity and love.

THE MAN WHO IS IN LOVE

You soon get to diagnose his symptoms, and it takes very little tact to draw out his story. His wounded heart yearns for the balm of sympathy. I have listened to so many love tales, and read so many love letters during these months that I now feel an expert in the science. Really one very

The Valley of the Shadow

quickly acquires the art of discerning accurately the position of your confidant. Has he been cruelly jilted, or has some misunderstanding which a word can put right arisen, or is he the victim of morbid fancies, or is the hand of the mischief-maker to be detected? A little practice and you are soon able to answer these questions right off. What plots for romance have been suggested as real life unbared its tragedies —and sometimes its comedies!

All these letters and talks have defined for me one face ugly as Satan, despite the hypocrisy of smiles, with eyes that cannot look straight, and with lines of cunning that blend into those of cruelty. It is the face of the mischief-maker whose foul game is to make sport out of the miseries of others. The mental depravity of the mischief-maker I can never understand. Unfortunately he or she—I fear most frequently the latter —has drifted into the nefarious pastime unconsciously. Possibly they tasted blood with their first sweet morsel of gossip, and their moral downfall has been quicker and

The Valley of the Shadow

lower than that of the drunkard. The morbid craving has enslaved them, and they have become a pest to society. I never knew what beasts of prey they were until I saw the marks of their teeth and claws on our suffering soldiers. Deeper and more ghastly than the wounds of the Turk are the injuries they inflict on the hearts of their victims. It is all done so simply and apparently so innocently. If I were a dictator at present I would round up all the mischief-makers and shoot them as traitors. Dante, I think, consigned them to the punishment of having their lips sewed together with thread. But then Dante was too kind; he had not been a chaplain, and listened to the heart agonies of men who, exiled from home, felt powerless to undo the evil.

Their letters have a wonderful sameness. They are generally from a cousin, a sister-in-law, or candid friend, and the remark is thrown in casually that the writer has seen Mary Jane with so-and-so, and that they were very thick and something more.

A CORNER IN PIETA CEMETERY

The Valley of the Shadow

Mary Jane being, of course, the girl to whom the soldier is engaged. Now, a man who is lying on a bed of fever or pain has generally lost the sense of humour. He takes things very seriously, and as he has little to think about except this bit of news which he has got from home, he turns it over and over in his mind until it festers. The doctor wonders why his temperature goes up, and one day it is the chaplain who discovers the cause. In a confidential mood the sufferer tells his trouble to sympathetic ears, and the chaplain who has had experience very soon sees that he is on the trail of another mischief-maker, and would like to wire home for her instant arrest, only our laws do not reach the real culprits.

Now, if these were isolated cases, I would not have wasted a page on them, but, looking back on my year here, and recalling my conversations with the men, I see how largely this topic bulks. Perhaps our wise women at home can bring kindly pressure to bear on all letter-writers, especially to our wounded, to avoid subjects that would irritate or arouse suspicions. The man in love forms a big percentage of our fighting force, and his special difficulties require delicate handling.

THE THOUGHTFUL YOUTH

There is a class of young man which grows impatient at the kind of mental pabulum considered by friends at home to be just the thing for wounded men. I do not say this class is large, but I fear that it is not being catered for.

"I want something to make me think," a young man said to me one day, when I asked him what he would like to read. I wished then that I had some popular histories or good biographies, or religious books that were readable, that did not hide great truths under a ponderous weight of learning which is apt to make sentences top-heavy, but books in which truth was put in simple and attractive form so that the reader assimilated it, and was not aware that the thoughts conveyed were profound until they began to ferment in his own brain and made him think. There is need for such in our hospital wards, where the mind is healthy and craves for food though the body may be suffering.

Some youths of this class came to me the other day. They were finding time heavy on their hands, and wished to put their idle moments to best advantage. So I suggested that I would teach them French. It would be useful for them when they returned to the Front in France, and in order that they might have the best of all text-books to study I chose the New Testament in French, and have sent home for sufficient copies. Future kind donors might perhaps take the hint and remember this special class, which is one that will repay any effort spent on it.

THE GRATEFUL MAN

Some of the remarks which our seriously wounded make unconsciously reveals the spirit of the Briton. I asked one man

The Valley of the Shadow

whose body had been mangled by a shell if he were in much pain.

" Yes, when I think of it," he answered.

Another whose leg was off and who had a bad wound in his back replied, " I might be much worse, like that poor chap down there who has lost his arm."

Mr. Cowan tells of a soldier who had a wound through his chest, and who could breathe only with great difficulty. This was not his only wound, for the bullet had first of all passed through his wrist.

" It was a lucky thing I got that wound," said the sufferer, pointing to his bandaged arm. "The surgeon tells me that by passing through my wrist the bullet got cleaned, and therefore the chest wound is not so dangerous as it would otherwise be." There are always two ways of looking at even a misfortune. Happy the man who has the knack of seeing it from the standpoint of gratitude. The experience of our hospitals is that our soldiers practise that art, and it greatly assists in their cure.

One day in passing through a ward Mr.

The Valley of the Shadow

Cowan saw a patient with a crucifix hanging above his bed. The man was a Roman Catholic, and both his arms were badly shattered, and stretched out in "cradles." The thought suggested was natural, and the chaplain could not refrain from remarking that the crucifix had its reflection on the bed.

" Yes, sir, but my suffering was nothing to His ; it comforts me to think that the Lord knows it all, and understands the pain, and if He does not remove it He gives me strength to bear it."

THE VALLEY

But I wished to take you just a little way into the Valley with me that you might see with what brave firm steps our heroes pass from us. Where there are so many incidents to relate I hardly know which to select. Let me choose the very latest, a bedside I visited yesterday evening. I had been spending four hours in Floriana Hospital, and it was after seven o'clock, and I was leaving a ward with the intention

The Valley of the Shadow

of going home, when suddenly I heard a faint voice say :

"Oh, Chaplain, speak to me."

I stopped and turned, and in the second bed saw a white boyish face. I went over, and the lad put his hand out and grasped mine, and held on.

"I am not afraid," he said. "Only I would like you to speak to me about God and pray with me. I have to undergo an operation."

Quietly in a few words I tried to picture to him the compassionate Christ and tell him of the door opened by the Cross. As I went on I became conscious that there were other listeners, and looking round saw standing quietly behind me Colonel Symonds, the surgical expert, with other two surgeons and nurses. He had motioned to them not to interrupt. When he saw that I had noticed him he touched me on the sleeve, and whispered,

"Go on, we will wait. It will be a very serious operation. One leg at least will have to come off."

The Valley of the Shadow

That sidelight into the sympathy of that great surgeon touched me much. His time was precious. His day had no doubt been a very busy one, and the hour was late, yet he would not seek to shorten these last minutes of spiritual consolation. I prayed with the lad, and he held my hand all the time. Poor dear boy, what he needed that moment was a mother's tender touch. He was about to sacrifice limb and perhaps life for our sakes, and he so young and gentle. Can we ever prove ourselves worthy as a nation of such sublime offerings?

On returning home four yellow envelopes lay on my table. I knew what these meant, for these are the August days when death is knocking constantly at the door. Three were intimations of men seriously ill, and could be left over until the morning. The other was a dangerous case, which I knew from sad experience meant that the man was dying. He must be seen at once. Perhaps he wished a will made out, a last message conveyed to loved ones. At all events he needed a word of comfort, the grip of a human hand to steady his footsteps in the Valley of the Shadow.

Shall I take you into the secret confidence of that solemn moment? Will it be breaking trust with the dead? Something I will keep back, but there is something I will tell, without name, and in words that are true to the spirit of the scene if not exactly to the letter.

"Where do you come from?" I asked.

He mentioned a parish in Scotland which I knew. When I said so a glad light came into his eye, and a faint colour warmed the pallid cheeks.

"D'ye ken the hoose on the hill a wee bittie aboune the kirk, that's my faither's?"

"Yes, and I know this that he will be praying for you to-night."

"An' my mither tae—an—an—Mary. Dae ye ken her? She's no twalve yet, but she's the cleverest girl i' the pairish."

He was thinking of his sister of whom he was so fond.

"I will give them all your love, and tell

The Valley of the Shadow

them that you will be waiting for them—yonder."

He was silent a moment. He understood my meaning, but Scottish reticence about spiritual things sealed his lips.

"Ay," was all he said, but it came from the heart, and was accompanied by the glitter of a tear in the eye.

"You have had a good father, but there is a better One waiting to welcome you. He has opened the door of His home for you, and stands ready to receive you. Will you not be glad to see your Saviour face to face?"

"Ay."

"Do you know Him?"

"Ay."

Then the reticence gave way, and the dying lad made his first confession.

"He spoke to me the ither nicht. I was alane on guard i' the trenches, an' He seemed a' o' a sudden to come that close, an' His eyes were fu' o' tenderness an' He asked me if I loved Him."

"And what did you say?"

The Valley of the Shadow

" Just ' ay,' but I meant it, sir."

I thought of Christ's words, "Let your conversation be yea, yea," and knew that the monosyllable was more than enough.

Such is a glimpse of the Valley of the Shadow as seen in our hospital wards ; and, as one by one our dying men pass beyond the range of human voice and touch to encounter the last grim enemy, I seem to hear the refrain of the hymn they loved, and used to sing so lustily :

> Onward, Christian soldiers,
> Marching as to war,
> With the cross of Jesus
> Going on before.
> Christ, the royal Master,
> Leads against the foe ;
> Forward into battle,
> See ! His banners go.

CHAPTER IX

A SCOTTISH PICNIC

MY typewriter and I have not kept tryst with you for some weeks. We have just been shoving along through the pile of letters that faced us, and did not feel justified in taking a morning off; for it is a recreation and pleasure to spend a few hours with Greenock friends, even though it be through the medium of a typewriter.

These weeks have not been idle; indeed, they have been so full of thrilling and touching events that I do not know where to start, and I hope you will allow me to ramble, for this is

A LETTER, NOT AN ARTICLE.

There is a subtle difference; in the latter you are master of your words, you choose

A Scottish Picnic

them with deliberation, and affix with effort the arrow point on to the shaft of the sentence ; but in a letter you let the words master you, you allow them to carry you whither they will. When you start you do not know where you are going, and you have no need for arrow-heads for you have no target. Of course it presupposes a most indulgent and sympathetic mood on the part of the reader. I feel somehow I may take that for granted this morning, for of your sympathetic interest I have been so assured that I will venture a trial of your patience. The real reason why I choose this method is that I have no imagination left. I have been spending hours in filling up the monthly army schedules of my staff, and my mind has got so entangled with red tape that it is bound hard and fast, and can only think in terms of forms, and were I to attempt an article there would be no spring in it, and it would be fit only for the waste-paper basket.

Speaking of letters : might I explain to you the method of our correspondence, as it will interest a large number who have written me. If the person enquired about is known, or can be found in Malta, a reply to the enquiry is sent at once ; if, as is the case in 90 per cent. of the letters received, we do not know about the person, then the name is put on a list for further enquiries, and it may take a long time before any information can be obtained, if indeed that is possible. So I trust that my correspondents will exercise patience, knowing that no enquiry is overlooked, and that all will be done to discover any news of the missing, and that silence simply means that there is nothing to write.

MALTA SIGHTS

Malta insists upon doing a little of her own nursing, and right cleverly does she do it. She has a panorama of interesting views with which to soothe the eye. I will not speak of her appeals to the ear and the nose. They have been greatly over-emphasised by other writers, and besides after

A Scottish Picnic

iodine and other things even street smells are a relief.

The man who is able to limp on his crutches as far as the Porte Reale is soon made to forget his pains. Perhaps nowhere in such little space is there such variety of costume or colour. He is soon as amused as a child looking at some fairy scene. It is a study in lights and shadows, for the sun is always blazing except when it is night. Here pass in review the dresses and clatter of all nations. Just now the prevailing colour is khaki, but there is always the background of black, for the faldetta is everywhere; and then there are the shovel-hatted priests, who are not few, and the bearded Capuchins, and the sailor ashore for a holiday, and the white uniforms of his officers, with the scenic effect of palaces and balconies, all of which fascinate the onlooker on this real cinema of life.

But he has only to take a step to vary the scene. Everything is so near in Valletta. Tired with the glare let him enter the cool, shaded stillness of St. John's

A Scottish Picnic

Church. At first his eyes can see nothing, so dazzled have they become with the blaze of sunshine. Then in the gloom of the great building he sees stationary figures every here and there. The faldettas of the women kneeling at prayer, looming indistinctly in the shadows, add to the sense of awe. Then, as he grows accustomed to the dimness, he begins to notice the gorgeous mosaic pavement on which he is standing, with its four hundred different armorial bearings, or he gazes at the rich altar, or walking across the nave, which is wider than that of St. Paul's Cathedral, he surveys the beautiful silver railings in the Chapel of Our Lady of Philermos, and smiles when he is told how Napoleon was cheated of his spoil by a coat of paint. When the French Emperor took possession of Malta he sought out its treasures, but the guardians of this precious silver railing made it look quite ordinary and worthless by a superficial daubing with paint, and it was passed by as of no account, just as often in life we miss seeing the consecrated in the commonplace.

A Scottish Picnic

Rev. William Cowan, who is the poet laureate of our staff, has expressed so well in the following lines the spirit of the place, that I cannot do better than quote them from his book, *Memories of Malta* :

ST. JOHN'S CHURCH, MALTA

> Enter, Oh stranger, through the curtained door ;
> Behold the altar girt with silver rail ;
> And tapestries which tell their sacred tale ;
> The tesselated splendour of the floor ;
> And chapels rich with treasure, where of yore
> In flowing robe, or clad in coat of mail,
> Repentant knights were wont their faults to vail
> 'Neath high resolve to go and sin no more !
> Deeming that Christian nations should unite
> In saving Christendom from that dark fear
> Which threatened Europe, zealous for the right,
> With consecrated shield and sword or spear,
> Beneath this roof they pledged themselves to fight
> For all that Christian manhood holds most dear.

But there are many other sights with which to beguile the idle moments. The armoury of the Palace with its four thousand pieces links the present to the past ; and, as you tread these ancestral halls and see the motionless figures armed cap-a-pie keeping their eternal vigil, you feel that you

A Scottish Picnic

are back in the company of the old knights and living in the classic days of Malta.

Malta, however, has a more ancient pedigree, and as the convalescent soldier is able to widen his circuit he can soon find himself in a much older world. The car will take him near to the Hypogeum, and as he descends to the rock-hewn vaults his fancy may hear the footsteps of a race whose weapons and implements were all of stone. Yet in their rude, rough way those stone-agers have done a service to the present generation. They have provided them with splendid bomb-proof shelters from the Zepps!

Haigar Kim is farther afield, but is worth the long drive to reach it. It means "Stone of Veneration"; and, as we stand in this centre of Baal worship, we might almost imagine ourselves back on the slopes of Carmel on that historic day when Elijah faced just similar stones and proved by miracle the vanity of their superstitious rites. Such ruins make more vivid the days of the Old Testament, and as we meet with the descendants of the ancient

Phœnicians, and Canaanites of Scripture, the Bible stories of boyhood become more real.

One great dome dominates the island, and somehow one never seems to lose sight of it. This is Musta Cathedral, and the dome is said to be the third largest in the world, its diameter being 118 feet. Its chief interest, in addition to the wonderful view secured from its summit, is the fact that it was built with the voluntary labour of the people of the village, who are now justly proud of their great church. On its steps you will always find some of our blue-jacketed convalescent lads, whose curiosity has been aroused by seeing its distant outline, and who do not leave the island without a pilgrimage to its shrine.

But it is of another pilgrimage I wish to tell you, and how it grew, and whither it went, and what it meant.

THE PICNIC FOR SCOTTISH SOLDIERS

A large number of our lads from Greenock, Glasgow, and the Clyde, who had passed

A Scottish Picnic

through our hands in the hospital wards, were about to take farewell of us and go back to the fighting line, so we determined to give them one day which they might remember with pleasure among the hard ones that lay before them. Mrs. Mackinnon suggested a picnic, and at first we thought of inviting only the members of those regiments connected with the Clyde district. But everything has a tendency to grow quickly here. I hardly know myself in these days, with my study turned into a Departmental Headquarters and with a staff that has grown from one to eight. It reminds me of the " down-east " Canadian farmer who sent his son west to seek his fortune with the advice, " Young man, grow with the country." Well, our picinc became infected with this spirit of growth. There are large numbers of Scotsmen recovering from the wounds of their first action, so we found that we could no longer limit our invitation, but had to include all Scottish soldiers. Then a company of Scottish nurses arrived on their way to

A Scottish Picnic

Serbia, and we thought that it would be nice for them to carry away a pleasant memory of Malta. Thus our picnic grew. Then we happened to visit the great camp at Ghain Tuffieha—it does not pronounce as it spells—and amongst the thousands there were many Scotsmen; were they to be left out? So our party grew and grew until on the eventful day it numbered 280. As befitted the occasion, the morning was Scotch. We had our first rain. Not the soft kindly drizzle of the West Coast, but something that reminded me of Greenock on a certain August day two years ago. It was complimentary of the elements, but there are compliments that one would rather dispense with. However, Malta cannot frown for long, and soon the sun was blazing again, the dust was laid and there was an attractive freshness in the air. The clouds had after all been weighted with blessing, as is the way with most clouds, if only we have the patience to wait. Long before the hour of departure a large crowd had gathered at King Edward's Avenue.

A Scottish Picnic

There also stood the forty brakes and carozzin—which is the plural for carozze. Some of the guests were on crutches, but looking very happy; others had an arm in a sling. The majority were once more in full khaki, which meant that they were ready to face the foe again. A happier crowd one could not wish to see, and their lightheartedness betokened the

TRUE SPIRIT OF OUR BRITISH SOLDIER.

The enemy has failed to damp that. It took much arranging to get them all seated, and then our long procession started off. From the distance, as it wended its way up hill and down dale, it might have seemed like a great funeral, were it not for the peals of hearty laughter and the outburst of song.

In order to make the drive instructive, a neat little leaflet had been prepared describing the sights of interest on the way. Malta is full of history. In fact at every turn one's imagination is carried back to the past, and you seem to live in a bygone age. Perhaps nowhere more so than when

A Scottish Picnic

you catch a glimpse of St. Paul's Bay, with the little island so accurately described in the book of Acts. Then we laboriously climbed the hill to Citta Vecchia. Passing through the walled gates of this ancient town one feels as if the twentieth century were left far behind in our return to the past. Then at the other side of the hill, after nine miles of a delightful drive, Boschetto suddenly unfolded its charms beneath us. On the left, in a commanding position, was seen Verdala Palace. The dignity of age rests well upon its solid masonry. The Grand Master Verdale built it in 1588. To-day it is modernised, and makes a fitting home for His Excellency the Governor. Beneath in the valley, down to which the Palace gardens slope, is a veritable Eden, just one little sheltered patch of green and shade in this parched land. Value is to a large extent a matter of contrast, hence Boschetto is a paradise to the Maltese. It might pass almost unnoticed in many a picturesque corner of the home land. My good fortune followed. It seems to be my happy lot in

A Scottish Picnic

life just to meet the right man at the right time. To how many such helpers have I been indebted ! Such a one is Mr. Chalmers of the firm of Messrs. Blackley—like his senior partner Mr. Morris, he has grudged no pains to facilitate our work for the wounded. On the occasion of the picnic he excelled himself. Under the shadow of the trees he had screened off with large Union Jacks a sheltered space where long tables were erected loaded with tempting eatables. I can reassure you that

THE REPAST WAS WORTHY OF GREENOCK.

The inroad of nearly 300 was an event in this secluded part of the island. His Excellency, the Governor, Lord Methuen, accompanied by his daughter, the Hon. Seymour Methuen, came to greet us. With much arranging we got some photographic views taken ; but, alas, like those of our hall last week, they have turned out a failure, except two taken while at table.

When at last we were seated at table, and had begun in the orthodox way of

A Scottish Picnic

Scotsmen by singing the second Paraphrase, and with prayer, His Excellency made a very happy speech, dwelling with tact on the prominent part Scotsmen were taking in the terrible struggle. I had an opportunity later of telling what Greenock was doing for the wounded, and I am glad that this has been reported in the local press.

After our meal games followed, and there was a general saunter round the place. It was now that one of the most extraordinary results of our picnic came about. There were cases of brothers meeting one another, the one not knowing that the other had been wounded or was in Malta, this being the first and only gathering of Scottish soldiers. In the crowd I ran against Stanley Lee of South Street, Greenock, who was in an Australian regiment. He did not know that his brother, Sergeant Lee, had been wounded and was on the island. Unfortunately it was too late for them now to meet, as the sergeant had returned to England. I heard also of four young fellows from the same workshop in Glasgow

A Scottish Picnic

meeting. They were all unaware that any of them had been in Malta.

All too quickly the shades of night began to fall, and we gathered once more in a large group and sang the Doxology. As I looked up and saw a star suddenly shine through the blue that was deepening into black, and looked on that mass of upturned, manly faces, and caught the swell of their song as it blended into a mighty chorus, " Praise God from Whom all blessings flow," I felt within the surge of a triumphant emotion. These men were bound to win, for theirs was the confidence of David, " The Lord of Hosts is with us ; the God of Jacob is our refuge."

CHAPTER X

UNDER CANVAS

MY title does not convey the whole truth, only half of me was really under canvas—my better half; the remainder was lodged in a hut; but all this needs explanation.

To most people, I suppose, Malta is thought of as a mere dot, or one big rock. I can see that this idea underlies the thoughts of many of my correspondents, who seem to think that I am within ten minutes of every hospital. But there are distances here as in other places, and I have just been inspecting some of the far-away camps—hence my title and my story.

Now, I am not going to mention names for various reasons: first, to reassure the Censor that no enemy, after reading this,

Under Canvas

will be any the wiser as to where the camps are which I have visited; and secondly, to spare your tongues, for the names are jaw-breaking, and I do not wish to cause you personal injury. It will be sufficient to know that they were " somewhere in Malta."

Although I am a true-blue Presbyterian, some of the duties of a bishop are falling to my lot; my flock is a scattered one, how scattered I did not fully realise until I took this tour. All our chaplains are keen and hard-working, but there are some corners, and those big ones, which even yet we have not turned, and as the responsibility of seeing that our soldiers are ministered to even in out-of-the-way places rests on me, I resolved to quiet my uneasy conscience by going to see for myself.

From one far-away camp a strange message reached me. It came from a wounded soldier who was lying there. He said he was glad, for the sake of the half-dozen Presbyterians in his tent, that the Senior Chaplain was coming, but all the men would

Under Canvas

be Presbyterians if the Chaplainess came too. So the Chaplainess packed her bag along with mine, and on a fine Saturday morning we left Valletta for our week-end in the country.

A very comfortable motor had been put at our disposal by the Government, so there was the zest of a holiday as well as the comfortable sense of doing one's duty, as we whizzed and tooted along the narrow roads.

Of sight-seeing as yet we have done very little, leaving it to the happier time when the first chimes of peace will sound cessation to our labours; yet if one carries open eyes almost every object here is a " sight." As we dived down into the valleys with their patchwork of fertile fields we caught glimpses of peasant life. Here we meet the original race in all the purity of their ancient Mediterranean blood. Last night I had a long talk with a Maltese officer who is an authority on the history of the island, and we discussed the sources of this unique people. A common belief is that they are

Under Canvas

the old Canaanites, whom Joshua drove out of Jericho, and certainly there is much to favour this supposition, as they are certainly allied with the Phœnicians. My friend, however, urged a more ancient pedigree, and tried to prove from skull measurements, as well as ancient inscriptions, that here we have the direct descendants of the "Mediterranean Man." He flourished certainly 4,000 years B.C., and if age confers honour on a race the Maltese have that claim. Like every people they have to be understood to discern their virtues, and the more one knows of them the more one discovers qualities to admire and honour. The passing tourist, who forms his opinions from the Carozze men, who cheat him, deceives himself and does discredit to his hosts. A patient, industrious people, who carry on a stubborn fight with Nature, is the verdict of the stranger who views their countryside. I would like to take some of those who talk wildly about the un-reclaimable land in our Scottish Highlands to the stone deserts in Malta, which have been made " to blossom as the rose" by pure industry. The very soil in some places has been imported, and every inch of ground round the rocks, that are too big to be moved, is cultivated with care. If we followed the example of the Maltese our waste lands would support a teeming population.

The people in the country differ from those in the towns. They are simple and retiring, and many, I am told, spend their whole life without ever having been in the streets of Valletta. Here we saw the heavy-limbed oxen at work, and the women with their hoes bending over their task. We had got far from the tinkle of the goat bells, which are heard in the streets. We dashed through little towns whose lanes were built on the zig-zag principle of the modern trench, and perhaps for the same purpose of defence. At last, after all the sensation of a rough day at sea, we slid down the last hill, swung round the last curve, and there stretched out before us a great array of tents.

Under Canvas

A HOSPITABLE WELCOME

The kindness received during our weekend visit to this camp is beyond words. Officers and Sisters have made it a memorable one. The home of the soldiers is to be found in a great Y.M.C.A. tent, which has been erected in the middle of the camp. This tent is but a part of the wonderful man who is its centre. It seems only a short time ago since one morning there called for me in Valletta a young man whose personality impressed me from the start of our acquaintance. He had just arrived with a large tent, and I was able to put him in touch with the right officers. Now all know him, and in that short time he has won in a remarkable way the esteem and confidence of all, from His Excellency the Governor to the private soldier, who has found in him not merely a sympathetic but a practical friend and helper. It does credit to the Y.M.C.A. authorities that they discovered the exceptional talents which Mr. Wilson possesses for the work to which

Under Canvas

they have set him. The officers, Sisters, and men in this great camp told me privately how much Mr. Wilson's coming had meant for them all, and there was universal sorrow when a telegram was received yesterday sending him to the Front. He is certainly the right man for that more heroic venture, but I doubt the wisdom of the Y.M.C.A. in taking him away from a centre where his influence for good has become so great. He possesses that subtle blending of sympathy, kindness, and firmness. He invites trust because there is strength and judgment in his decisions.

The officers had got up an "afternoon tea" for us, and in their quarters a long table was spread. The Sisters who nurse in the tent hospitals were invited, and a very happy party we all made. I found many Irish, several Scottish, and some Canadian doctors on the Staff. They naturally feel a bit shut out in this distant camp, but the isolation has compensations. The air was delightful, and the view of rugged

PIETA CEMETERY WHERE THOSE WHO DIED OF WOUNDS OR SICKNESS IN THE GALLIPOLI CAMPAIGN ARE BURIED

Under Canvas

cliffs and deep blue sea was restful after the narrow streets of Valletta.

The Sisters' quarters are a little way from the main camp. A Scottish lady—of course—is Matron, and one feels proud of one's country on being introduced to Miss M'Dougall. She is one of those matrons of whom you are not afraid, and yet she rules with a firm hand; but she has that touch of sympathy which evokes the loyalty and love of those on her staff.

One of the latter I must mention, for it is well that those at home should know something about the nurses to whose hands their sons are entrusted. This lady is also—of course—Scottish, although born in Canada; but she can speak Gaelic. So wise in judgment and shrewd in her knowledge of human nature, and withal possessed of such a big heart, that the needs of others seem to be her one thought! Such is this Miss M'Gregor, and such are some of those brave women who, in their self-sacrificing service, show to the world the true charm of noble womanhood. From such hands

Under Canvas

our laddies receive a mother's care, as well as the skill of the latest scientific training.

The Sisters sleep in bell tents; a larger marquee had just been erected in their grounds to contain seven beds, and Mrs. Mackinnon had the honour of opening it and being its first occupant. So now you will understand the enigma of my first sentence. I had a bed in one of the officers' huts, so that my title "Under Canvas" does not really apply to me, but to my better half!

A SUNDAY IN CAMP

In the blistering heat of August I miscalled the weather of Malta. True, these days are not so very far away; only last week we had a sirocco, which caused every one to perspire in the same old midsummer fashion. But Sunday made up for it all. There was plenty of sunshine, but the breeze seemed to have the suspicion of a nip in it, so much so that some of our Argylls in a confidential moment hinted to Mrs. Mackinnon that singlets would be a

Under Canvas

great boon, and at this present moment she is busy purchasing some for them. Possibly if the nip becomes a little more acute the need may be intensified. I know how quick Greenockians are to take hints, perhaps they might give this a thought. Up to the present the very idea of heavier clothing has been an oppression, but the climate, like other things in the Eastern Mediterranean, is a bit fickle.

The morning parade service was conducted by the Anglican chaplain. It took place in the open, the clergyman and officers alone being on a sheltered stage. It was an inspiring sight to look into the faces of a thousand men. Many were about to go back to the firing line, and would be spending the following Sunday face to face with death. I may say in passing that the relations between the Presbyterian and Anglican chaplains are most friendly. Naturally where there are many camps and hospitals, and many services to arrange, there must be a brotherly spirit of give and take, and so far all difficulties have been surmounted in a spirit of kindly co-operation.

After service, as there were a few hours to spare, and the morning is not a good time for visiting the tents, Mrs. Mackinnon and I were tempted to take a walk. I am not going to say how many miles it was to St. Paul's Bay. To a Greenock minister whose work has developed the right kind of muscles it means just half the distance that it is to others. The invigorating air, the bright sunshine, and the interesting objects en route made the way seem short. On the hillsides we saw cave dwellings still inhabited as they were four thousand years ago. Then we descended to one of the few real beaches in Malta. Here bays are still called creeks, and as we sat where the wavelets broke on the sand the scene in the book of Acts was vividly pictured to us.

"When it was day they knew not the land; but discovered a certain creek with a shore, into which they were minded, if it were possible, to thrust in the ship. And falling into a place where two seas met, they ran the ship aground."

In front of us was clearly visible the place where the " two seas met." A little island divides the waters at the entrance of the bay, and round this the waves swirl in a storm, and their meeting churns the surface into foam.

A monument marks the traditional place of the landing, and there is every reason to credit the site. As I sat there I felt the centuries bridged. The eyes that had looked on the vision of the Crucified had looked also on this spot, which is little changed. There was a sermon in the thought.

That afternoon we went through the hospitals, and had a word and gift for all our Scotch lads. Also in the tents I had some delightful chats with men whose thoughts naturally turned to the homeland. Here again I met Sergeant Lee's brother, of South Street, also Sergeant Leggatt, whom I had last seen at St. David's, while Mrs. Mackinnon was surrounded with

Under Canvas

a crowd of those who when nearer Valletta used to frequent the Reading Room and enjoy the Greenock teas. The afternoon passed all too quickly.

At 6.30 p.m. I conducted the service in the big Y.M.C.A. tent, and the sight was an inspiring one. Seats were provided for about 500, but every inch of standing ground was also occupied, and round the doors as far as one could see the men crowded. I thought, as I looked into those earnest faces, of the loafers on our streets at home to whom the church bells mean nothing. What a rebuke to them there was in that audience if only they could have seen it! One's pride in our soldiers increases daily. To them religion is a reality, and if only these men are spared to return to the homeland the day of the moral weakling will be past.

But there, I have exhausted my space, and not even finished the story of a day. I would like to have told you of some of the officers I met in the Mess. One, a major interested me greatly, and we talked on

Under Canvas

long after the lamp had burned itself out and left us in darkness. He is one of the few old regular officers left, and had been all through the retreat from Mons, and the subsequent battles. Our conversation left me very optimistic. He said in decisive tones that Germany was already hopelessly beaten. On this consolation I slept soundly. On the following morning the motor was waiting, and we said good-bye to our new friends in that isolated camp with feelings of gratitude for all their kindness.

CHAPTER XI

CHRISTMAS IN MALTA

CHRISTMAS has been casting, not its shadow, but its sunshine in advance over the wards of our hospitals. The ceilings were the first to catch its glow. From their heights festoons of crimson-and-white and every rainbow hue began to hang their graceful loops, and the men who could look up from their beds caught the gladness of their message.

CHRISTMAS AS A HEALER

The reflection of Christmas first crept over the wan faces of the sufferers as they watched the festoons grow. There was something now to look at, where there had been bare walls before. Interest for the eye is a factor in healing that is often overlooked.

Christmas in Malta

For instance, the other day I was in one of our hospitals, the windows of which look out on the Grand Harbour. As I stood by the bedside of a wounded man the view attracted me. A fringe of curling surf lined the breakwater where the Mediterranean swell, like some other things, was kept at arm's length from the sheltered waters within. At that moment a big battleship was making her way slowly outward. With her snake-like tail, armed with its two stings, she suggested an ocean reptile as she crept through the waters, and she almost seemed to twist her trailing body as she swung through the narrow channel.

"You cannot weary here," I remarked thoughtlessly. The man's bed, which was on the opposite side of the ward, faced the window, and for the moment I imagined he also could see the harbour. "Sky and ceiling is all that I have had to look at for these weeks," he responded. I lowered my head to the height of his pillow, and realised the truth of his words. If his bed had been raised just a few inches he would have had a reserved seat in one of the most picturesque and natural cinemas of the world.

Christmas has given our patients something else to look at than bare walls. In fact, these can hardly be seen now, so covered are they with decorations. Mottoes, festoons, crowns, bells, and a hundred other old fancies have been worked out of the same material—ordinary tissue paper of every colour,—until the stock in Malta has run short. The lettering of white wool was in some cases glued on to cardboard by jam instead of gum, or by the remains of certain milk puddings, which some of the men said made excellent sticking paste.

In one ward I was impressed by the unity of design. Nothing was out of keeping with the dominant chaste idea. There were no mottoes hung haphazard, no over-elaboration of one section of the room to the disadvantage of the other. In fact, only one central inscription was allowed, and that was "God Save the King." On

Christmas in Malta

enquiring for the master mind that had the strength of character to impress his individual design on all the others, I found it beneath the bed-clothes. In one cot lay a man badly wounded, but his brains were unimpaired, and from the blankets he dictated his commands to the willing workers who had recognised his genius. His absorption in his work made him forget his pain, and the Christmas joy had no purer reflection than on the face of the artist, as from his pillow he surveyed with admiration the working out of his own designs.

In another ward the chief adornment was an excellent model of the Lord Nelson, made in cardboard by one of the crew. Perhaps the busiest man in Malta that day was his Excellency the Governor, Lord Methuen, as he sped in his car from hospital to hospital, with words of appreciation and encouragement. Next to him should be ranked the nurses, doctors, and chaplains, amongst whom there were no idle hands.

Christmas in Malta

GIFTS

Thanks to the hampers received we were able to give a present to fully three hundred Scottish soldiers. Mrs. Mackinnon had these done up in suitable small parcels, and Sassenachs wished that they had been born in the Land of the Open Hand.

Many a fair Santa Claus had filled the socks she had made with something to eat as well as to wear. For there were little boxes of chocolate hidden in the toes. Here was something to warm the heart as well as the feet and brace the courage. Pinned on one pair was a slip of paper with this verse written in a girlish hand :—

> When ye are hidin' ahint the rocks,
> Think o' the lassie wha made these socks.

Tea outside! It sounds strange for Christmas. Yet on the balconies of most of the hospitals long tables were spread, fairy lights hanging from above cast their glow over plates filled with cakes; and the doctors, traitors for once to their own

Christmas in Malta

profession, actually assisted in handing to their patients what on other occasions they would have forbidden with a frown. But then, that is the way of Christmas, and its truce seems to be extended not merely to the minds and hearts of men, but to certain internal organs, which usually are only too ready to prove querulous on the slightest excuse. At all events, I was told by several Sisters that temperatures were not up on the day succeeding.

MALTA WEATHER

The best and most appreciated gift was that sent to Malta by the "Clerk of the Weather." From a series of delightful days he chose the choicest. The clear atmosphere, bringing near objects miles away; the bright sunshine, that warmed but did not overheat; the suspicion of a nip in the air—all made Malta a different place from those August days, when every limb was weighted, and the only place to escape from liquidation was in a cold water bath, and even then, though submerged,

Christmas in Malta

one had a grave misgiving that he was perspiring still.

The weather had its own Christmas decorations, and I never saw finer. It reserved the best for the sunset hour; then Nature began to hang up her fairy lights. What colouring there was in the sky! The deep blue merging into dark purple towards the horizon, and the sea, as if vieing with the heavens, changed to green. I never suspected Nature of being a suffragette before, until she brought out her Christmas ornaments and advertised her sentiments in colour. Only for a few minutes she held us spellbound; then she rang down the curtain of night. But now her real illuminations were only beginning. I have seen stars in the dim distance before. That moment she brought them near at hand. Looking down from one's roof that night at the lights of the town shining so clearly, at the lights on the harbour which made the waters seem alive as dghaisas, like fireflies, skimmed the surface of the sea; and then, looking up from man's limitations

Christmas in Malta

at God's lights, one felt that the symbol for Christmas was rightly a star.

Later on we returned to Valletta Hospital to be introduced to Father Christmas. Very patriarchal he was as he marched through the wards, and his violin solo took the audience in one of them by storm. His Scottish reel made the men without legs painfully realise their loss. There was something very familiar about his accent when he spoke, though I do not think that even the United Free Church people of Banchory would have recognised their minister. They may be assured that Rev. Wm. Cowan is putting his talents to splendid service for the welfare of the wounded, and in his own parish of hospitals has won the hearts of the men under his charge. "Padre," the soldiers' term, is the best word for the chaplain. It expresses that quality which elicits the confidences of the men. Strange and touching are the stories we often have to listen to, and sometimes the services we are asked to perform are most confidential and delicate. I have been

Christmas in Malta

very fortunate in having as colleagues men who have proved genuine "Padres," and we only wish that our expressed desire for the return of Rev. Donald Campbell had been gratified. His whole-hearted services here are not forgotten. Just yesterday I met a New Zealander who had returned to Malta wounded for the second time, and whose first enquiry was for the Greenock Padre who had been so kind to him at Floriana in June.

THE SCOTTISH TEAROOM

I could take you through endless wards where men are fighting pain with the grim determination of the battlefield; but there is one centre of goodwill which you should know about, if not take an interest in. Scotland has been belying in Malta the character which those who are ignorant of her give her. She will be known in far Australia and New Zealand as long as the tale of Malta's hospitals are retold as the Land of the Open Hand. The Mother Country has revealed a mother's heart and

Christmas in Malta

care towards her sons of Empire. Six months ago our Scottish hall was opened in Valletta, and every day has been a Christmas there, as far as gifts are concerned. A table has been spread daily for the hungry boys, who, having found their limbs again, have also suddenly re-discovered their appetites.

If you know what enteric is, then you will know what it means to be hungry, and you will not consider two teas in an afternoon an extravagance—the one in the hospital, made by an orderly, and the one in this "hame frae hame," where ladies handle the teapot with that gracious skill which adds an indefinable flavour to the tea.

They come into this little hall from the ends of the earth. The Australian, with his easy stride; the New Zealander, who is a fine compromise between the Scotch and colonial character; the Newfoundlander, thick-set and square-shouldered; the Irishman, who is an inch taller since the Dublin Fusiliers said with their rifles and bayonets

Christmas in Malta

to Bulgaria "Stand back"; the English, the Welsh, and our own laddies; and not least the dark-skinned sons of India, who drink their tea, and who must needs march to the kitchen and salaam to the ladies by way of thanks. From 400 to 500 a day they have come, and Scotland bids them welcome. A cup of tea is not much in itself, but an essay could be written on all that is inside and around it; and so it is always Christmas Day in this little hall.

CHRISTMAS TRAGEDY

But the season did not pass without a reminder that the angels' song was falling on deafened ears. Into our service on the Sunday night walked twenty dusky Cingalese. Their ship, the Ville de la Ciotat, had just been submarined by the enemy. They gathered round me at the close, and told me their story. This Christmas they will remember not for its joy and goodwill, but for its hatred and inhuman cruelty. Instead of the angels' song, they heard that day the mocking laughter of men who

Christmas in Malta

jeered at their despair. Without a warning their ship was struck as they were sitting at a meal. At 15 knots an hour she plunged to her watery grave, and in those few minutes when hands gripped hurriedly the lowering tackle of the boats all rushed on deck. One of the life-boats filled with women and children capsized, and the occupants were thrown into the water and drowned.

One of the men told me how he jumped into a boat which immediately afterwards was smashed against the ship's side. Grasping a rope he hauled himself once more on deck, just in time to be carried with the final plunge of the ship into the waves, from which he was rescued at last by friendly hands. In suspicious tones they spoke of two foreign steamers which had been in their vicinity shortly before the attack took place. In high praise they referred to the captain of a British ship, which came to their rescue while the wake of the submarine was still plainly visible ; and on this boat they were brought to Malta. And after a

Christmas in Malta

meal these twenty Cingalese sought out the Presbyterian Church, and were in time to join in our evening service. They were sad at heart, for they had lost nearly half their comrades; but, as I looked into their swarthy faces, I felt proud that British khaki clothed such heroes.

NEW YEAR

The celebration of New Year's Day was different. It was more purely Scottish. "It is a capital arrangement," said one of the garrison officers to me. "On Christmas Day I turn out a Scottish guard to look after the other chaps, and on New Year we set the English to watch the Scottish."

There was a touch of home about New Year's Day, with its morning church service and opportunity for good wishes. For night we had arranged a big social for the St. Andrew's unit of the R.A.M.C. In passing let me pay a deserved tribute to this splendid body of men. I have come much in contact with them, and know how exacting their work is. "Orderly!

Christmas in Malta

orderly!" How that call is for ever echoing through our wards, as some poor fellow in pain calls for help. Also I find that this corps are apt to be overlooked. Hence we reserved New Year's night for them. The hall was packed, and we had a real Scottish soiree. Our youngest and most versatile chaplain, Rev. Charles McEchern of Tighnabrualich, was in his happiest mood, and with song and story he helped to make the evening a merry one. "I wish we could have a whole evening of him" was what I heard one man remarking. What choruses we had! Staff Sergeant Lee taught us all in five minutes how to imitate the bagpipes; and I am quite sure even a hundred pipers an' a' could never give such a startling blast or weird drone as lips and lungs produced that night. Too quickly the hours sped, and the strains of "Auld Lang Syne" fell on the midnight air, and the little bit of Scotland resolved itself into Malta once again.

Christmas in Malta

VISITING THE ARGYLLS

Now I have a feeling that I am not getting into the right swing of this letter. There are many causes, the hour is late, and the day has been a busy one ; but, when I tell you that it has been spent in visiting the Argylls in the various hospitals, I know I have secured your interest without literary wiles, and your pardon for slipshod expressions and heavy sentences.

About thirty Argylls have just come in, so I have devoted a day in trying to see them. Let me tell you how I got on. I started in the motor-car immediately after lunch. I had a call to make at Verdala Palace, which is near Boschetto of picnic fame, and my Jehu seemed to realise that I had to put thirty visits into the afternoon, for we took the corners of narrow streets at perilous angles, and when we did get a bit of straight road we hardly seemed to touch the surface. After leaving Verdala Palace we had to cross nearly half the island to reach St. Patrick's Camp. Skirting Citta

Christmas in Malta

Vecchia, we dived down into numerous little villages, bringing momentary consternation into groups of children, mule-drivers with their carts, and goats. But my driver, I saw, had a good eye for the fraction of an inch, so I gave faith its opportunity.

We drew up at St. Patrick's Camp. The first Argyll I found was Kemp, who was quickly recovering from his encounter with a Turkish "coalbox." He offered to be my guide in my search for the other Argylls, and was of great assistance. In tent H 3 I found also M'Leod, who seemed in the best of spirits despite the bullet wound in his arm. How brave our boys are! Next I spoke to Donelly, M'Gilvray, and Leimon, about whom their friends need have no anxiety. All seemed glad to see me, and the few *Telegraphs* I had soon disappeared. Then we crossed over to another row of tents, and I had a nice chat with Richard Hamilton, who was lying in bed. He is doing well, though somewhat weak. He had been buried in earth by a shell. From

Christmas in Malta

there we crossed over to visit Gray, who is able to go about. Then we walked to the very top of the camp and found M'Cartney and N. Adam. The former, who was a chum of David M'Dougall in the trenches, had been told that I would be sure to look him up when he arrived in Malta, so he was expecting me, and I am glad that I acted up to expectations. After a little search we discovered H. Robertson, who is moving about, and at last Simpson, who has been flitting from one tent to another. His eye is getting quickly better. So with regard to the Argylls at St. Patrick's I can give a good report. Kemp accompanied me back to my car, carrying my bag, which was now nearly emptied of its contents, and I started with a farewell wave to H 3, where the Argylls were standing.

My next camp was St. David's. We had a cross-country journey to it, through lanes that would make Devonshire ones seem thoroughfares in comparison. It was lucky we met no cart or mule on the way— lucky for them I mean, and after many

Christmas in Malta

sharp turnings we slowed down as we ran into St. David's. We take a paternal interest in this camp; for it is here that we have pitched our tent. I can remember it in its babyhood, with its swaddling clothes of mud and little else. Now it is a "castrum" worthy of Roman soldiers. Fine roads have been made through it, well paved and firm; and most wonderful of all, it has prettily laid out gardens with flowers blooming and vegetables ripening. Truly, the desert has been made to blossom as a rose. In its centre stands the United Free Church Guild Tent, a stately ornament of canvas. Useful, too, for within are large numbers of men sitting at tables reading or playing games. In this camp I found T. Fisher. He also will soon be convalescent.

Then I boarded my car again, and went on to All Saints' Camp. Here a considerable search was required before I discovered W. R. Stewart. He was looking splendid. Now the car was turned homewards, but we stopped at St. Andrew's Hospital to

Christmas in Malta

make two calls. Here I found J. Currie of the Argylls, who was down with enteric. But it is a mild case, and gives no cause for alarm. A friend of Rev. Donald Campbell's lay in another block, named Millar, and I dropped in to give him a word of cheer. He is progressing slowly.

When I regained my car I looked at my watch with a start. How the afternoon flies out here, especially when you are talking to Greenockians! At that moment I was timed to speak at a meeting some miles away. But I had faith in my Jehu, and he did not disappoint me. I arrived at the Scotch Church Hall in Sliema in the nick of time. The chairman was just going to announce that I had not come when I walked in. Here the glow of the New Year lingered. Rev. W. Cowan was giving a Scotch social to his parishioners. He had brought them from the different hospitals in his parish to that hall, and he had commandeered my wife to make tea. About 120 Scottish wounded were present. A good tea had been provided, and the men

Christmas in Malta

looked too happy to be bored with much speechifying, so I told them just what you have all been thinking, how proud you were of all of them.

Now I am afraid that I have bored you with these commonplace incidents of a chaplain's day, which is just like so many others. Only I know that to some it will not seem commonplace, for it has reference to their brave sons; and I wish those at home to feel what I have told the men here, that while they are in Malta they are to look upon me as a "Padre" in the real sense, one who will father them, and on Mrs. Mackinnon, to whom I find they tell their needs more readily than to me, as one who will stand in the place of their mother. They are a family we are proud of, noble fellows!

AN ARGYLL'S FUNERAL

Yet my report—for that is what my letter has become—is not to be without its sad note. Private Gordon Smith (2947) died of his wounds at St. Elmo Hospital on Saturday, a few hours after being admitted. His home address is 14, Serpentine Walk, Greenock. The first announcement I got of his arrival was the news of his death. He had been badly wounded. His funeral took place on Sunday afternoon, and though it was not my turn for funeral duty that week I arranged to take it, feeling that his friends in Greenock might prefer that one from their own town should lay their hero to rest.

I closed my Bible Class half an hour sooner, and drove to the cemetery in good time. As I stood robed at the gate my thoughts were in Greenock. I felt that I must be the eyes for the friends there. I hope to send you shortly a photo of Pieta, where now more than one Greenockian lies. Then from the Porte de Bomb there broke on the quietness of the Sunday afternoon the beat of a drum, slow, mournful; and soon I could see coming down the tree-shaded street the gun carriage with its burden. As the procession turned the corner and moved to the gate, and the soldiers took their stand with rifles reversed,

Christmas in Malta

I stepped forth to meet my fellow townsman, glad that Greenock had its representative that day. Silently his comrades in arms bore him to his last resting-place. The Presbyterian service allows latitude, and so there were many things in my prayers that moment which the bystanders might not understand; but He whose eye rests on the home by the Clyde, as well as on the carnage of war, will answer with His own consolations the petitions by the open grave. So we left this heroic son of Greenock with the echo of the parting volleys, and the Last Post, in our ears; and he left with us a bequest, the greatest of all heritages, the example of noble self-sacrifice and heroic achievement.

CHAPTER XII

RELIGIOUS WORK AMONGST THE WOUNDED

WHAT about the ultimate results of all the war work in Malta? I do not now refer to the mere mending of limbs, the giving of a good time to the patients while they sojourned here. That has of course absorbed a great deal of the energy of the workers on the island. But though this phase of local activities is the one naturally most evident, has there not been something accomplished which is less transient? I think so. There has been Empire building of an enduring kind.

The fact that nearly one hundred thousand youths at the most impressionable period in their lives, with spiritual instincts quickened by the perils of the battlefield, have had time for meditation forced upon them, has not been lost sight of by those whose special care is the development of Christian character.

The men who have passed through our hospital wards have come into touch with spiritual influences, and as we part with many of our patients, who go back to rejoin their regiments, the farewell hand-grip, the word of gratitude bespeak the stirring of the soul's deeper feeling.

HARMONY

His Excellency the Governor, in his foreword to this volume, has very wisely emphasised two striking features of the work in Malta, *harmony* and *co-operation*. This has been true of every department, and particularly so of religious work. The Senior Chaplain of the Church of England, Rev. M. Tobias, who has now gone to the Front, was a man of such breadth of sympathy and genial manner, and sound common sense that friction in co-operation with him was an impossibility. This is true also of the Rev. Peverley Dodd, the Wesleyan

Religious Work Amongst the Wounded

Senior Chaplain, whose aim in life seems to be to smooth the way for others, and most successful he is in it. Not only does he carry on his ministerial duties, but superintends the Connaught Home, a large institution for soldiers and sailors which has proved of great service during these war days.

Rev. C. Harker, the Senior Roman Catholic chaplain, has also co-operated in a most brotherly fashion in common effort, and in their varied duties the different chaplains have always sought to assist one another by forwarding to the right quarter the names of any soldiers they came across who wished to see their own chaplain. Thus the work has been made easier for all.

This feeling of good fellowship has certainly received inspiration from the headquarters of all denominations, the A.A.G.'s sanctum. Major Howard-Vyse, the military officer responsible for the Chaplains' Department, has handled his team with great skill. If he were an ecclesiastic, I would suggest him as the most suitable

INTERIOR OF RECREATION TENT.

Photo by Chrietien & Co., Malta.

Religious Work Amongst the Wounded

man for effecting union amongst all the churches. After his success in Malta advocates of union should keep their eyes on him. They might do worse than take a few leaves out of his book.

RELIGIOUS RESULTS

So much for organisation, now for fruits. During the year we have had three special evangelistic missions amongst the men with very gratifying results. In May the Church of England chaplain, along with Rev. Donald Campbell and Rev. G. A. Sim, started a series of meetings in Imtarfa Hospital. These were splendidly attended, and struck a key-note that has distinguished that hospital during all these months. The responsive audience here is always like a bath to the soul. What is left of us after an eight miles' journey in the heat and a busy day may be very limp. But standing on a platform in a hall where practically every chair is occupied, and men sing, with an intensity I have never heard before, " I need Thee every hour," makes

Religious Work Amongst the Wounded

one forget all physical weakness, and I never turn homeward without a strange gladness in my heart. Such is the effect that certain congregations have on the preachers, and I have noticed that every chaplain who ministers in turn at Imtarfa becomes infected with the religious buoyancy of the place; and though they being new-comers may not know it, I trace the results back to those stirring evenings when the first wounded men from Gallipoli confessed so earnestly their faith in Christ. Nearly a hundred of them came forward with the old request, " Put down my name, sir," as they enrolled themselves under the Banner of the Cross. That generation quickly passed away, a few weeks at most was the length of each man's stay. Mr. Campbell, the gracious fragrance of whose ministry still seems to me to linger round these beds, in due time also left, but the blessing remained. The new audiences still sing the old hymns made sacred by those first nights of consecration. Staff-Sergeant Fryer alone is left now to recall

Religious Work Amongst the Wounded

those moving moments when men in tens gave themselves to God ; and, as his voice rings out the notes of the familiar hymns that upbore the souls of those men to the Throne of Grace, I catch the echo of those days. Many of the men who made confession then had returned to their regiments to take part in the battles of the subsequent months, and to-day they are no longer seeing through a glass darkly but face to face.

Who can take stock of the steady work of the chaplain as he goes in and out through those death-shadowed wards ? Just as you cannot identify the special ear of corn in the harvest field that sprouted from a particular seed, so it is not possible to recognise the fruit of much that seems very commonplace service. As Senior Chaplain I have been very fortunate in my colleagues, who accepted the tradition of hard work joyfully. I do not think I overdrew for them the picture of Mr. Campbell's faithfulness, going forth after breakfast with eager feet laden with literature and

Religious Work Amongst the Wounded

Testaments for the wounded, returning with dragging footsteps for lunch, and setting out immediately afterwards on the same errand, because he could not think of "those poor dear boys passing a night in their pain without a prayer, a hand-grip, a word of comfort." So he set the pace and outdid his own strength, but left an example that has stimulated his successors.

Rev. Alex Macinnes, one of our chaplains, has put his experience in the following words:—

"We have seen the men in various camps and in different stages of their training; the raw recruit, with wonder and surprise in his eyes, depression and sometimes rebellious thoughts in his heart; the trained soldier, strong, equipped, disciplined, intelligent; the men leaving in drafts for the Front, smiling to disguise their not unmanly tears, wondering what experiences awaited them, trusting, many of them in the protecting love of the Father God. But in Malta we saw *sick* men, and all our previous experiences seemed to go for

Religious Work Amongst the Wounded

nothing : sick men, after the privation and suffering of the Peninsula. Let it be said right away that we never met one discourteous man, one unbeliever, one sceptic. All of these may have been there. We never met them. The sick soldier seems to have no use for scepticism. It might amuse him in civil life ; not in Malta. All of them were willing to speak about religious matters, the soul, the Saviour, Eternal life, naturally and easily. It seemed to be the main thing to speak about. Some asked me to pray with them. All said that they would like me to pray when we suggested it. On Sabbath how fine our meetings were ! The men usually chose the hymns, ' Come away boys, shout out the numbers.' Whatever the *four* might be, 'Jesus, Lover of my Soul,' and ' Rock of Ages ' were always there. Rarely did we hold a service but some lad or lads waited behind to talk. They would tell of the Bible Classes they had attended, the Church, or Mission Hall, the Choir in which they had sung. Such experiences were most helpful and encouraging. Many of the lads confessed that they had lost their grip of the Unseen; but they were anxious to re-enlist in the Army of Jesus Christ. Yes, the Spirit of God was at work. The men had had time to think. They had looked into the face of death. They had seen their companions falling by their side. They had realised their own miraculous escape. They had been brought back from the gates of death. God's merciful guardianship was over them, and they knew it. Some of them, it must be confessed, changed not for the better when they became stronger; but these were few. God has done a gracious work in the hearts of all of them, and many of them left St. David's Camp and the Tent which they loved next to their own home realising that the Saviour was a real Person, the most real Person in all the world."

I can only speak of the great moments when men confessed their faith in such numbers that all took note. Such another movement took place at Ricasoli. Again all the chaplains of the different denominations united. Mr. Menzies was our representative, as it was in his " parish." I always listen with delight to his preaching; but that Wednesday night, when the marquee was packed with wounded men and his words about sin went home, I felt the responsive throb-beat of that big audience as never before. There were quiet Scottish lads there, who at home were shy about religion, who now with tears in their eyes and unashamed made open confession of their loyalty to Christ. One feels these scenes are almost too sacred to be written about, yet it is right that the world should know the manner of man we have sent to our trenches, and not accept a caricature of the British soldier as the conventional type. We have seen that type; but we have also seen the boyish laddie who dared to go down on his knees to his Maker, and the bronzed sergeant who faced unflinchingly a packed tent to tell the " old, old story." The men of Ricasoli have separated, but I feel sure that as long as they live they will not forget those nights. The net was again cast, and

Religious Work Amongst the Wounded

sixty or seventy made open confession of their faith.

Judging by numbers, the biggest success in our work was that obtained in our third series of meetings which were held in the large camp at Ghain Tuffieha. Here again all the denominations united, though the Rev. J. A. Kaye, the United Board Chaplain, and the Rev. W. L. Levack of Leuchars were the soul of the movement. It was in the days before the Orkney hut, and the big Y.M.C.A. tent was put at our disposal. Every night for a week it was crammed to the last inch of standing room. No preacher could desire a more inspiring audience. The array of eager young faces that confronted the speaker fanned his fervour. These are the men who after the war are going to set the world right, and one felt that they were in the right kind of preparatory school for that task. Hardship and danger like cruel pick-axes were breaking the fallow ground of their hearts, and now was the moment for sowing the good seed. Aptly was it scattered in those furrows,

Religious Work Amongst the Wounded

and the result that was immediately manifest, great though it was, could only be a fraction of the spiritual good done. It strengthened one's own faith to see how interested these young men were in the things that pertain to the soul.

War has its degrading influences, but it has also its quickening agencies. Men think as never before when confronted by eternity, and never once in all my experience have I met a wounded soldier who resented any reference to religion. In fact I have found it nearly always welcomed.

Strange and sometimes almost amusing are the arguments that impress. The other day I met a man who let me know with some pride that he was an agnostic. I might say that he had not been at the Front and smelt powder, but had been dropped off in Malta as an invalid on the way out. I have always found that those who have been under fire are much easier of access. In fact, after a few minutes' conversation, though no reference has been made to the subject, one can usually guess correctly whether they have been to Gallipoli or not.

The patient I refer to took me in hand from the start, and expounded evolution to me in tones that admitted of no contradiction.

"The whole universe has evolved itself, and we are entirely the product of our environment," he said. "There is no place in it for religion."

"In fact we are the helpless victims of natural law," I added.

"Yes, natural law is pitiless. Mercy is a thing it does not know. It is unalterable."

"But how about its exceptions?" I asked.

"Exceptions?" he queried, looking a little puzzled. Then he added with emphasis, "It knows nothing about exceptions."

"The law, for instance, that heat expands is rigid," I said.

"Yes."

"If that were so," I continued, "ice would then be formed at the bottom of our seas, where no summer sun could reach it, and pile itself up with successive winters until all our lakes and oceans would be filled with ice and the earth become uninhabitable. Your law of heat expansion required an exception to make life possible. Below 32 degrees it is cold that expands. Who made that exception? Someone surely who is greater than the law, and who is merciful to mortals."

It was an old, simple argument that I hesitated about producing, yet it torpedoed this man's reasoning. I left him with the query, and when I returned some days later he said,

"I cannot get that exception out of my thoughts. Some higher power has certainly interfered with the law of heat."

"But it is only the Author of the law that has the right to amend it and He has done it in love."

From that day the man was very silent, and I saw that he was thinking deeply. What the result was I had not the means of knowing for he passed on.

Religious Work Amongst the Wounded

BIBLE DISTRIBUTION

The National Bible Society of Scotland has been one of our best helpers, and put into our hands "the sword of the Spirit, which is the Word of God." Three thousand copies have been sent to us free of charge, and these we have handed to the wounded. Had I time and space I might recount many interesting stories of these Testaments. Let me mention two.

Here is a touching incident told to Rev. Donald Campbell by a wounded Glasgow Australian lying in the Valletta hospital. On Mr. Campbell asking if he had a Testament, he replied, "Yes, here is a Bible that I picked up on the field of battle near Gaba Tepe." Then he produced a well-bound copy of the Scriptures of the Oxford type, bearing the inscription, "To Harry from his mother. The Lord watch between me and thee when we are absent the one from the other, 17/9/14," and expressing the hope that he would be brought home safely to her. Close beside the Bible a letter from the

Religious Work Amongst the Wounded

mother was lying, which the soldier had taken possession of. From it he learned the full name of the "Harry" of the inscription. He expressed his confident hope to be able to restore the Bible to the mother of the young Australian who, he feared, had fallen in action.

Another interesting story was also told the same day by a private of the Royal Scots. He showed Mr. Campbell a Bible through which a bullet had passed and been diverted, thus saving his life. He said that he had received this copy from Miss Ewing, daughter of Dr. Ewing of the Grange, Edinburgh.

Y.M.C.A. WORK

Malta has afforded another illustration of the perfect organisation of the Y.M.C.A. Under the energetic guidance of Mr. Wilson, its pioneer worker on the island, equipment and staff soon kept pace with the sudden increase of camps and hospitals. In October, 1915, the first marquee was erected at St. Paul's Camp, and in November the

Religious Work Amongst the Wounded

larger one in All Saints' Camp. At the same time the largest tent, a 90-foot marquee, was set up in Ghain Tuffieha Camp. His Excellency the Governor at the opening of these tents spoke with warm appreciation of the Y.M.C.A.

The religious element has been kept in the foreground. Every day closes with a gathering of the men for family worship. Their attitude at these moments is the best indication that a spiritual as well as a social need is being supplied. There is no impatience, no grumbling if games are interrupted for that purpose. An air of reverence at once pervades the scene, talking ceases and heads are bowed as an account of the day is rendered to God.

The opportunity for educating the minds of the convalescents has not been overlooked. Historical and general lectures have proved very popular, and Lieut. Laferla, a Maltese officer, has done much by his lectures to inform the men concerning the history and customs of Malta.

Religious Work Amongst the Wounded

Subjects suggested by the War, such as "The Growth and Power of the German Empire," have greatly interested the audiences.

Mr. T. B. Wheeler succeeded Mr. W. T. Wilson, and he brought to completion the work that was started by his predecessor. Soon he had eight large tents erected at different centres, and he developed the work in many ways. One of these was in catering for the musical tastes of the men. Male voice choirs were formed, and at Ghain Tuffieha Camp a splendid orchestra was organised, the instruments being provided by the Countess of Chesterfield's Ladies Auxiliary Committee. But the greatest success was that scored by Miss Lena Ashwell's Concert Party, whose services offered by the Y.M.C.A. were gratefully accepted by His Excellency the Governor, and the echoes of one of their songs still seem to haunt the island with their blood-curdling thrill! Altogether this party gave one hundred concerts.

Mr. Wheeler soon got erected two large

Religious Work Amongst the Wounded

Recreation Huts. One is situated in St. Patrick's Camp, and has proved itself a welcome centre for the men. Perhaps the hot climate of Malta makes these rooms even more acceptable than elsewhere. In the tent the air grows suffocating by midday; outside it is even worse, and it is like stepping into a hot oven to venture out; but in the Recreation Hut there is comparative coolness. Hence it is filled. The other hut has recently been erected at Ghain Tuffieha. It is a gift from the people of the Orkney Islands, and is worthy of its donors. Scotland in this has showed itself again "The Land of the Open Hand," and Malta can never forget the generous part played by it in ministering to the sick and wounded.

The Hut, which is a large one, capable of seating five hundred men, was shipped to Malta in sections, and erected by the convalescents in that camp of the unpronounceable name but of happy signification, "Valley of the Apple." Fully equipped for reading, writing and games,

Religious Work Amongst the Wounded

with an elegant stage and capacious refreshment bar, it has already proved an immense boon to the men busy with trying to get fit again. Already the grateful recipients of the gift have laid out the surroundings in gardens and attractive approaches.

Thus has the Y.M.C.A. faced its task in Malta. The practical sympathy of His Excellency the Governor has done much to make the work easier. His gift of the suite of rooms in the Palace Buildings for a Y.M.C.A. Headquarters has proved most valuable. The staff of about thirty has done its part well, one whose services have been greatly appreciated being Mrs. Holman Hunt, the widow of the famous painter. But without the organising brain and energy of a good leader the present success could not have been attained. When Mr. Wilson left every earnest worker in the island felt that the loss was great; and now that Mr. Wheeler has chosen the sterner part of fighting in the trenches instead of ministry, the community, while admiring

Religious Work Amongst the Wounded

his patriotism, feels that the force of a strong and wise personality will be sorely missed. He is succeeded by Mr. Lewis, who has already won the confidence of all. Thus in its selection of agents the Y.M.C.A. has been most fortunate.

All the chaplains and religious workers in Malta have been greatly encouraged and helped in their work by the sympathy and ready assistance of His Excellency the Governor. A motor was placed at their service, and where there were so many camps and outlying garrisons this proved invaluable. Rev. W. Cowan had taken with him a wonderful little lantern with a light whose brilliancy was out of all proportion to its size, and he had also an assortment of slides fit to draw tears to the eyes of every homesick Scot. There was not a fort on the island at which British troops were stationed which had not its "Night in Bonnie Scotland." Over fifty such lectures were delivered, and it was often near midnight when we rumbled back

Religious Work Amongst the Wounded

into Valletta through deserted streets in our car.

His Excellency was seconded in all his efforts for the good of the men by Lady Methuen. She has been ever quick to devise means for adding to the comfort of the wounded and in caring for the large number of young men for whom Valletta has its temptations. Her graciousness and the esteem which she has earned in Malta make her assistance in any endeavour a source of great strength and success, and ungrudgingly has she given such support to all religious and social effort.

Thus have the hands of the workers been upheld, and the way made easy for them; and though the memory of the past year is haunted with its nightmare and the vision of the glazing eyes and drawn features can never be forgotten, across its dark background there shines a wonderful rainbow. Malta has added a bright chapter to human history, and with reverence will its hospitals ever be named; for there sacrifice has once more been enthroned, and unself-

Religious Work Amongst the Wounded

ishness garbed in nurse's cape or surgeon's uniform proclaimed the triumph of love; and there might be heard for those who had ears to hear the footsteps of the Great Physician.

Lightning Source UK Ltd.
Milton Keynes UK
UKHW011852161221
395765UK00001B/237